Budapest

Budapest

Original Text:	Paul Murphy
Updated by:	Neil Schlecht
Photography:	Neil Schlecht; Byron Russell (pages 69, 70, 72, 74, 75, 84, 95, 97 and 99)
Cover Photography:	Neil Schlecht
Editorial/design:	Dial House Publishing Services Ltd
Cartography:	Raffaele De Gennaro
Managing Editor:	Tony Halliday

First Edition 2002 (Reprinted 2003)

CONTACTING THE EDITORS
Every effort has been made to provide accurate information in this publication, but changes are inevitable. The publisher cannot be responsible for any resulting loss, inconvenience or injury. We would appreciate it if readers would call our attention to any errors or outdated information by contacting Berlitz Publishing, PO Box 7910, London SE1 1WE, England. Fax: (44) 20 7403 0290; e-mail: berlitz@apaguide.co.uk; www.berlitzpublishing.com

Printed in Singapore by Insight Print Services (Pte) Ltd, 38 Joo Koon Road, Singapore 628990. Tel: (65) 6865-1600. Fax: (65) 6861-6438

Berlitz Trademark Reg. U.S. Patent Office and other countries. Marca Registrada. Used under licence from the Berlitz Investment Corporation

060/301 RP

CONTENTS

● A ☛ in the text denotes a highly recommended sight

Budapest

BUDAPEST AND THE HUNGARIANS

Budapest is split right through by the great River Danube, like a hyphen in the city's very name. Just as the Danube divides Europe into East and West, so it divides this city's west-bank Buda district from the east-bank district of Pest.

East and west, the city has been tugged in both directions for almost its entire history. In the opening lines of Bram Stoker's *Dracula* (1897), an English visitor arriving in the Hungarian capital feels a sense of foreboding as he "leaves the West and enters the East." Having emerged from four decades of Soviet rule — only the most recent in a long series of conquests, occupations and frustrated uprisings — Budapest may now be more "Western" than ever. Yet its newfound openness and cosmopolitanism compete with still-palpable reminders of its Eastern heritage.

The largest city in Central Europe, Budapest is also one of its loveliest, hugging the curve of a wide bend in the Danube. Along the west bank, the city climbs quickly up to Castle Hill, site of the former Royal Palace, and the medieval village of Buda. Over a period of 800 years, Castle Hill suffered 31 sieges and was reduced to rubble on numerous occasions. Yet enough has survived for it to remain one of Europe's most charming medieval enclaves.

On a flat, low-lying plain across the river is Pest, the modern administrative and commercial hub of the city, which grew to prominence in the 19th and early 20th centuries. An admirable example of town planning, the so-called Inner City is distinguished by broad, leafy boulevards, continental cafés and handsome baroque, neo-classical and art nouveau buildings. The city's grand, *fin-de-siècle* look

Art-nouveau details enliven many of the city's façades.

has prompted many to call Budapest "the Paris of the East."

The point where the two sides face each other, across the Danube, is what defines Budapest best. Lining the left bank of Pest is the palatial neo-Gothic Parliament building, a whole city block of white spires, topped by a neo-Renaissance red dome. Just as famous is the 19th-century Chain Bridge, regally guarded by four stone lions and linking (along with seven other bridges) the two banks of the city.

The story of how Budapest came to be is a tale of two or, more accurately, three cities. Until 1873, there was no such thing as Budapest — only the three towns of Buda, Pest, and Óbuda (Old Buda), all separate and distinct, though fast encroaching upon one other. Allowing for this technicality, Budapest ranks as one of Europe's youngest capitals.

In fact the city's history can be traced back thousands of years, pre-dating even the arrival of the Romans. They set up an outpost in the first century A.D. (in present-day Óbuda, in the hills just north of the Castle District) to defend their empire against so-called barbarians (meaning "bearded ones") from the east. When the Roman Empire eventually crumbled, successive waves of these barbarians, including the Huns and Avars, invaded and settled the land.

At the end of the ninth century, the Magyar nation arose out of this conflict and chaos. By the 15th century, Buda had become a rich center of learning and culture, crowned by the formidable Hungarian Royal Palace. However, invasion, occupation, war and destruction then ravaged the people of Budapest for the next 350 years. The city repeatedly emerged from disarray only to succumb again.

The city's 20th-century fortunes were scarcely more happy. Twice Hungary entered a world war on the losing side, with devastating effects. In 1948 the Soviets imposed their rule on a fractured land, crushing a popular uprising eight years later. Hungary was ultimately the first Eastern European country to make holes in the Iron Curtain — quite literally, by tearing down the barbed-wire border separating the country from Austria in 1989. That act began a momentous chain of events that finally brought an end to the Communist domination of Central and Eastern Europe.

Today, Hungary is poised to enter the European Union on a fast track, along with the Czech Republic, Poland, and Estonia. Budapest, the capital, abounds with conspicuous signs of Westernization and newfound private wealth, where there were once mostly hammers and sickles and state-owned businesses. BMWs and Volkswagens are replacing the old Trabants and Skodas on the streets. Young people crowd into American fast-food outlets and fashionable bars, speaking fluent English or German into their cell phones.

Few overt reminders of the former Soviet presence remain on the streets of Budapest. Avenues, streets and squares have had the political orthodoxy struck from their names, and the larger-than-life statues of Lenin, Marx and heroic Communist workers have been discreetly tucked away in a remote Statue Park, where they are a powerful and bizarre reminder of Cold War days.

With a population of 2 million, Budapest — home to 20 percent of the Hungarian people and 10 times the size of Hungary's next biggest town — thoroughly dominates the country in all aspects. It is Hungary's political, industrial, economic and cultural hub. For foreign visitors, Budapest is also the country's best attraction.

The Hungarian people, and their famously complex language, remain something of a mystery to the other, mostly Slavic, peoples of Central Europe. No one is really certain how or where the language developed. Linguists have identified some common but distant roots with Finnish, but doubts and disparate theories remain. Even so, you're unlikely to be plagued by language problems in Budapest. English and German have almost entirely displaced the Russian that Hungarians were obligated to study in school under Soviet rule.

Budapest has a vibrancy some visitors might not expect in a former Eastern-bloc capital. The city pulsates with noise from bars and casinos, and classical and Hungarian folk music are both enthusiastically supported in Budapest — the city that produced such world-famous composers as Franz Liszt (1811–1886), Béla Bartók (1881–1945) and Zoltán Kodály (1882–1967).

Civic enthusiasm reaches its apex at the city's thermal baths. Budapest is built above more than 100 natural hot springs, and the city's thermal baths — which range from domed Turkish baths unchanged since medieval times to art nouveau palaces — are world-renowned. Locals bathe in hot mineral waters for pleasure as well as for medicinal purposes, as they have for generations. Visitors can join Budapestis who soak and socialize (and even play chess waist-deep in steaming waters) — and a spa holiday in Budapest will cost a great deal less than in other parts of Europe, or in North America.

Hungarian cuisine is famous for hearty goulash, delicious pastries, and the liberal use of paprika, but it is not limited to those standards. Like everything else, dining out in Budapest has changed dramatically in the past decade. During the 1980s, the government retreated from its monopoly on restaurants, and the uninspired cooking of the Communist canteen is now largely a thing of the past. Several of Budapest's traditional restaurants are famed in Central Europe, and a handful rate among the best in Europe. Charming restaurants with Hungarian and international (and even vegetarian) menus have opened all over the city.

Budapest is the primary destination of most visitors to Hungary, but the capital is ideally positioned for day trips into the countryside. You can bike or take a cable car to the Buda Hills, prized for exhilarating views and fresh air, while only slightly farther afield are the charming old towns of the Danube Bend. Szentendre, the first of the towns along the great river, is a charming artists' colony with an 18th-century feel and hordes of summer visitors. Visegrád and Esztergom, just slightly farther along the Danube, retain more in the way of ancient treasures, including the remains of formidable medieval castles and palaces, as well as the country's largest cathedral and its finest religious art collection.

The favorite holiday spot of many Hungarians lies a couple of hour's journey southwest of the capital. Lake Balaton is Central Europe's largest lake and the best approximation to the sea that this land-locked country possesses. The lake has something for just about everyone, though it is sharply divided in character: the south

Relaxing at the public bath is a way of life in Budapest.

shore caters overwhelmingly to families, while the north abounds in activities for outdoor and culture enthusiasts.

But wherever you venture in Hungary, you're never far from the capital, either physically or mentally. Budapest has made great strides to shake off its Soviet shadow and take control of its destiny. The city has reawakened to find itself in modern Europe, and even as Hungarians race enthusiastically to catch up with their Western counterparts, they retain a proud sense of their past — evidence of the stubborn progress of a nation and of the resilience of its people.

Modern sculptures, like this one in Leopold Town, have replaced Communist-era statues in many parts of the city.

A BRIEF HISTORY

A nomadic tribe known as the Magyars, setting out from the region between the Volga River and the Ural Mountains, migrated to the Carpathian Basin towards the end of the ninth century A.D. and here they established a lasting base. When the leader of the Magyars embraced Christianity and his son István — better known to the world as St. Stephen — was crowned first king of Hungary on the symbolic date of Christmas Day, 1000, the Hungarian nation was born. By European standards, then, Hungarians are relative newcomers. Their 1,000-year struggle to become a prosperous and independent nation is marked by a cycle of invasion, foreign domination and revolt.

Early Settlers

Human presence in present-day Hungary can be traced back hundreds of thousands of years. Less than 65 km (40 miles) west of Budapest, human traces thought to be half a million years old have been excavated and are now on display at the Hungarian National Museum (see page 49).

Around the third century B.C. a Celtic-Illyrian tribe known as the Eraviscans, refugees from wars in Greece, occupied the area of today's Budapest. They established a tribal capital on top of Gellért Hill and a settlement in Óbuda, which they called Ak Ink (meaning "Ample Water").

The Roman Empire

Hungary remained beyond the reach of Western Europe until the first century A.D., when the Roman Empire's legions advanced and pushed its northeastern frontier to the Danube River. By the second century, 20,000 Roman troops had been deployed along the river between Vienna and Budapest.

Archaeologists have uncovered the substantial remains of Budapest's Roman predecessor, the city of Aquincum.

To command and coordinate this long and exposed line, the Romans built a military camp called Aquincum. This became home to 6,000 soldiers and eventually spawned civilian suburbs housing up to ten times that number of people. In A.D. 106 Aquincum was made the capital of the Roman province of Lower Pannonia. The sheer size and quality of the remains unearthed in present-day Óbuda testify to the importance of that Roman settlement, with its thermal bathing complexes, aqueducts, and places of entertainment.

As the Roman Empire began to crumble, Huns and Vandals crossed the river from the east and laid siege to the settlement. Commanded by the notorious Attila the Hun, these tribes succeeded in capturing Aquincum in the fifth century. The town the Huns established on the west side of the river was named after Attila's brother (or possibly his brother-in-law), Buda, who was banished there. When the powerful Attila died in 453, the Avars overthrew the Huns to become the dominant power in the region, occupying it from the middle of the sixth century to the early ninth century.

The First Hungarians

The first tribes to settle permanently in the region arrived in the late ninth century, having migrated a long way from their home east of the Ural Mountains. These tribes were called Magyars, and the name stuck for both the country and the people's language. Related tribes, who had earlier traveled northwest while the Magyars migrated west, ended up in Finland and Estonia. Their difficult and only distantly related tongues are classified together by linguists as Finno-Ugric.

The first military leader of the Magyars, Prince Árpád, founded a dynasty that lasted more than three centuries and introduced statehood to the new land. Prince Géza, his great-grandson, embraced Christianity, and on Christmas Day A.D. 1000, Géza's son, István — later Szent István (St. Stephen) — was crowned the first king of Hungary in the town of Esztergom, situated on the Danube Bend. King Stephen I built churches and transformed Hungary into a new Christian nation.

A landmark of the nation's civilization in these early days was the Golden Bull of 1222, a "Magyar Carta" spelling out the rights of nobles and commoners alike. But human rights were the last thing on the minds of the Mongols, who overran the country in 1241 and again in 1242. Whole towns and villages, including Buda and Pest, were devastated by an orgy of killing and destruction. The Mongols retreated, however, and King Béla IV set about restoring the wrecked nation, wisely constructing the rebuilt town of Buda within fortified walls.

The Angevin Dynasty

The Arpád dynasty ended in 1301, and the French House of Angevin (Anjou), in the person of Károly Róbert (Charles Robert), claimed the crown. He moved the court to Visegrád before it came permanently to Buda's Castle Hill.

Two more foreign kings ruled after Róbert, though it was a Hungarian nobleman from Transylvania, János Hunyadi, who became the national hero in the mid-15th century. The Ottoman Turks had been threatening the country for some time but Hunyadi led the Hungarian army to victory against them at Nándorfehérvár (now Belgrade) in 1456.

The son of János Hunyadi, Korvin Mátyás (Matthias Corvinus), ascended to the throne in 1458 and for the next 32 years, Hungary enjoyed a golden age of intellectual and civic development. Under this enlightened king's rule, the city of

A Magyar warrior stands guard outside the Museum of Applied Art.

Buda became the focus of the country's cultural renaissance, and Pest flourished as the hub of trade and industry. King Mátyás's newly built Royal Palace on Castle Hill was the talk of Europe.

King Mátyás died in 1490, having built Hungary into a great power. He failed to deal with the threat represented by the growing power of the Ottoman Turks on his doorstep, however. This time, when they attacked, there was no Hunyadi to lead the weakened nation. The king, Lajos (Louis) II, and much of his army were killed at the battle of Mohács (in southern Hungary) in 1526.

The Hapsburg rulers of next-door Austria, fearful that Vienna would be the Ottoman Empire's next conquest, proclaimed themselves rulers of Hungary to create a buffer zone between themselves and the Turks. Hungary was effectively dismembered, with the north and west falling to the Hapsburgs, Transylvania becoming a so-called independent principality under Turkish auspices, and central Hungary falling under direct Turkish rule. The Turkish occupation and the tripartite division of Hungary would last almost a century and a half, though the Turks left behind little of note except their thermal baths.

By the late 17th century, the Christian armies of the West were fully mobilized against the Ottoman infidels. Long, devastating sieges were laid to both Buda and Pest. They were finally liberated in 1686, but once again the cities lay in ruins.

Under the Hapsburgs

And still the Hungarians did not win their freedom. They were simply bounced from one empire to another, becoming subjects now of the Hapsburgs. In 1703 Prince Ferenc Rákóczi led an eight-year struggle for independence.

Outnumbered and deserted by their French allies, the Hungarians finally lost this war in 1711.

Peace lasted for the rest of the 18th century, and the country made great economic strides as a province of the Hapsburg's empire. Pest expanded its role in international trade while Buda regained its status as Hungary's administrative hub.

But prosperity was confined to a minority. Serfs got steadily poorer, and the Germanic Hapsburgs suppressed Magyar culture. In the mid-19th century, the Hungarians once again went to war for their independence. The rebellion of 1848 was led by a group of young intellectuals, including the 25-year-old radical poet, Sándor Petofi. They formed a short-lived provisional government, headed by Lajos Kossuth. The Emperor Franz Joseph I summoned help from the Tsar of Russia, and crushed the revolt in 1849.

The Pengő in Your Pocket

Although many people are aware of the crippling hyper-inflation that plagued Germany in the days after World War II, it isn't as well known that Hungary holds the dubious record for the world's worst inflation. The currency, known as the *pengő*, lost so much value that you needed to own 1.4 billion pengős after the war to achieve the same purchasing power as one pre-war pengő. In 1946 there were Hungarian bank notes in circulation worth a mind-boggling 10,000 trillion pengő.

Hungary also has the distinction of issuing the world's most worthless postage stamp. In 1946, a single British penny would have purchased 50,000 million of these 3,000-pengő stamps.

In 1867, a compromise designed to curtail home-rule agitation established the Austro-Hungarian Empire. This "Dual Monarchy" saw out the 19th century on a bright note, with the construction of splendid boulevards and proud buildings, including the Parliament building on the Pest side of the Danube. The Chain Bridge became the first permanent link across the river, the Pest metro system and the Pest-Vienna railway opened and, in 1873, the towns of Pest, Buda, and Óbuda finally merged to become the single great city of Budapest.

War and Revolution

In 1914, as a constituent part of the Austro-Hungarian Empire, Hungary had no choice but to enter World War I. The country's involvement in the war cost many thousands of Hungarian lives, and the country's hardships multiplied.

In October 1918, the Bourgeois Democratic Revolution toppled Hungary's last king, Károly IV. The revolutionaries joined with the nascent Hungarian Communist movement, but they took their reform demands too far and too fast, provoking a right-wing backlash, led by Miklós Horthy.

Meanwhile, the consequences of being on the losing side in the war were brought home to Hungary when the victorious Allies reduced the country to about a third of its pre-war size. Under the terms of the 1920 Treaty of Trianon, large areas of the country, including the homeland of Transylvania, were handed over to the new "Successor States" of Czechoslovakia, Yugoslavia, and Romania. Horthy maintained his role as regent in the grim 1920s and 30s while the country, demoralized and impoverished, seethed over the terms of the treaty.

Hitler's Germany, meanwhile, provided investment in Hungarian industry and a market for Hungarian farm produce, even earning a grudging admiration from the Hungarians for its defiance of the World War I allies. In 1940 Hungary allowed the German army to cross its territory. As a reward, they temporarily recovered lands from Romania and Yugoslavia. Soon, however, thousands of Hungarians were to die supporting Germany on the Russian Front, and when Horthy thought he could squirm out of Hitler's grasp by declaring neutrality in 1944, the Germans simply occupied the country.

In late 1944, the Soviet army was closing in on Budapest. Horthy played his last card by declaring an armistice. The Germans responded by imprisoning Horthy and handing power to a Hungarian fascist group called the Arrow Cross. This brutal and fanatical regime murdered hundreds of Budapestis and ensured further destruction of the city by fighting the Red Army to the death. During this period, as many as 500,000 Hungarian Jews were deported to the death camps at Auschwitz, Birkenau and Treblinka. By the time the Russians finally assumed control of Budapest, three-quarters of its buildings had been demolished and the Hungarian death toll in the war had reached half a million.

In and Out of the Red

Post-war Hungary was transformed from a republic in 1946 into a People's Republic three years later under Soviet rule. After a hopeful democratic beginning, Stalin's appointed leader, Mátyás Rákosi, established the sinister AVO secret police to ensure compliance with party doctrine, rooting out supposed "class enemies."

After eight years of state expropriation and brutal repression, 50,000 students and workers marched on parliament to air their grievances on 23 October 1956. Angry students toppled a giant statue of Stalin near Heroes' Square, and the police fired on protestors outside the Hungarian Radio headquarters. The protest snowballed into a potent popular uprising that drew worldwide attention. Within days a provisional Hungarian government, led by the reformer Imre Nagy, had withdrawn Hungary from the Warsaw Pact. Soviet retribution took just 12 days. On 4 November, Red Army tanks rolled into Budapest and quickly crushed the armed resistance. The West watched in horror as Nagy and thousands more were executed. Some 25,000 Hungarians died and another 200,000 fled the country.

The Soviets installed János Kádár as the new party boss. Although his rule began with repression, Soviet ideological and economic doctrines were more relaxed by the mid-1960s, and Kádár became an unlikely reformer. Hungarians embraced a limited form of consumerism, known locally as

"goulash socialism" and the country's economic performance was held up as a model to other states in the Eastern bloc, even though it failed to meet its potential. Even so, Hungarians were allowed to visit certain countries in the West, though limited to one trip every three or four years, and they enjoyed a measure of prosperity not seen in other Eastern bloc countries.

A new era dawned in Budapest's history with the ending of Communist rule.

As the winds of perestroika reached Budapest from Moscow, Kádár was removed from power in 1988. The following year the formation of opposition parties was legalized. Hungary then literally pierced the Iron Curtain by dismantling the barbed wire barrier along the Austrian border, allowing those who wanted to escape to the West. In 1990 the country held its first free elections in 43 years and again became a democratic republic. In 1991 Hungary became an associate member of the European Union and in 1999 Hungary was inducted into NATO. In 2000, Ferenc Mádl was sworn in as president.

In its transition from Communism to capitalism, Hungary has managed to gain a significant injection of Western investment to help support its fragile economy. Hungary's hopes for the future now include full membership in the European Union and the two things that have proved so elusive in the country's history: peace and freedom.

Budapesti schoolchildren learn about democracy on a visit to the Parliament building.

WHERE TO GO

The murky green Danube — more prosaic but no less significant than Strauss's famous Blue Danube — cuts straight through the heart of Budapest, neatly separating the medieval streets of Buda from the late 19th-century boulevards of Pest. History lovers will be drawn to the Buda side of the river, while keen shoppers, business visitors and night owls are likely to spend more time in lively Pest.

Orientation and getting around the city are rarely a problem; the majority of sights are crammed into the central areas. Castle Hill is tailor-made for walking, as are such Inner City boulevards as Andrássy út and the pedestrian-only Váci utca. Most parts of town are efficiently served by the metro (subway), or by buses and trams.

For the most part this chapter follows the natural layout of the city, starting on the western bank with Buda, then moving on to Óbuda and the hills, Pest on the opposite side of the river, and finally Margaret Island, just north of the Chain Bridge in the middle of the Danube. The best place to begin a tour of the city is Castle Hill.

CASTLE HILL (VARHEGY)

The fascinating district where the former Hungarian Royal Palace overlooks the Danube is the most picturesque spot in Budapest, and the best — or, more accurately, the only — clue as to how the medieval city once looked. Charming streets are lined with beautiful old buildings, and many houses bear plaques describing their history. As serene as it seems today (when not overrun by tour groups), the district was the site of countless waves of destruction visited upon the city by Turks, Hapsburgs, Nazis, and Soviets, and many places have been rebuilt more than once.

Highlights

All museums listed below are open from 10am to 6pm (closed Monday) and make a nominal admission charge.

PLACES

Castle Hill Old Town. Charming medieval streets and stunning views of the river and Pest from the battlements of the neo-Gothic Fishermen's Bastion. *Funicular railway from Clark Adam tér or Várbusz from Moszkva tér.* (See page 26).

City Park (Városliget). Lovely grassy park area; don't miss the splendid Széchenyi Baths (opening hours as Gellért Baths) or Vajdahunyad Castle by night. *Hosök tere, M1.* (See page 58)

Gellért Baths (Gellért fürdő). Splendid steam baths and pools in art nouveau building, plus beautiful outdoor pool with wave machine. *Kelenhegyi út 2-4; Tel. 466-6166.* Also of interest are the **Széchenyi** and **Király** baths. (See box on page 78 for hours and details of major thermal baths.)

Buda Hills. Serenity and plenty of greenery, with magnificent views and a chairlift ride (closed some Mondays). *Cog-wheel railway then "Children's Railway."* (See page 43)

Szentendre. Delightful 18th-century town and artists' community on the Danube Bend. Picturesque cobbled streets full of churches, museums, and art galleries. *HÉV train from Batthyány tér.* (See page 65)

Esztergom. Danube Bend town and spiritual hub of Hungary, with the country's biggest basilica and best collection of religious art. *Bus, boat, or hydrofoil from Budapest; bus or boat from Szentendre.* (See page 70)

BUILDINGS AND MUSEUMS

Royal Palace/Hungarian National Gallery (Magyar Nemzeti Galéria). Seven centuries of Hungarian art, from Gothic altars to Impressionist paintings. Contemporary international artists in the **Museum of Contemporary Art** (Múzeum Ludwig), *Wing A. Szent György tér 6 (Wings B, C,*

D, and A of the former Royal Palace); Tel. 375-7533. Funicular railway from Clark Adam tér. (See page 35)

Great Synagogue. The second largest in the world, dating from the 19th century, with the **Jewish Museum** in its annex, commemorating Jewish culture in Hungary, and the Holocaust. *Dohány utca 2-8; Tel. 342–1335. Open 10am-3pm. Closed Sat. Metro: Deák tér.* (See page 50)

Hungarian National Museum (Magyar Nemzeti Múzeum). Hungarian history from Roman times to the end of Communism; St. Stephen's cloak is here, but the crown jewels have been moved to the Houses of Parliament. *Múzeum körút. 14-16, Tel. 339-2122. Metro: Kálvin tér (M3).* (See page 49)

Houses of Parliament (Országház). The massive neo-Gothic 19th-century building echoes its counterpart in London. Opulent halls. *Kossuth Lajos tér, 1-3. Guided tours daily in English at 10am and 2pm, German at 11am and French at 2pm. Metro: M2.* (See page 52)

Museum of Fine Arts (Szépmuvészti Múzeum). Ancient Greek, Egyptian, and Roman relics; Renaissance paintings and Old Masters, including a great Spanish collection; 19th-century art. *Hősök tere; Tel. 343-9759. Metro: M1.* (See page 57)

Museum of Applied Arts (Iparművészeti Múzeum). Arab-themed 1896 art nouveau building housing Hungarian arts and crafts exhibitions. *Üllői út 33-37. Tel. 217-5222. Metro: Ferenc körút (M3).* (See page 61)

Aquincum. Roman ruins and archaeological museum. *Szentendrei út 139; Tel. 368-4260. Ruins: 9am-5pm; museum: 10am-5pm, April 15 through October. Closed Monday. HÉV railway from Batthány tér to Aquincum.* (See page 41)

Skansen Open Air Village Museum (Szabadtéri Néprajzi Múzeum), near Szentendre. Rural buildings and interiors, occasionally staffed with actors to make a "living museum." *Szababság-forrás út; Tel. 26/312-304. Open 9am-5pm Tuesday to Sunday, April to October. HEV train to Szentendre then number 8 bus.* (See page 67)

The district overlooks the city from a long, narrow plateau divided into two sections. The southern part is occupied by the enormous former Royal Palace (where the original castle once stood). The northern district consists of the historic streets of the Old Town, or Vár, where 14th- and 15th-century aristocrats and artisans once rubbed shoulders.

From Pest there are various ways of getting up to Castle Hill. The most popular method is aboard the 19th-century funicular (*sikló*), which begins just beyond the end of the Chain Bridge, on the other side of the roundabout, and rises to the Royal Palace. Another option is to take the metro to Moszkva tér, climb the steps to the road, and catch the mini Várbusz service that shuttles to and from Dísz tér, stopping at numerous points en route. Or, you can simply walk up the hill using any one of several streets and staircases (cars are forbidden on the hill unless you are a resident or a guest at the Hilton Hotel).

Historic Streets: the Old Town

☛ **The Old Town** consists essentially of four streets running parallel to each other, packed with colorful burgher houses, historic monuments and small museums. A short walk to the right of the funicular terminus brings you to Dísz tér (Parade Square), which marks the start of the northern section of Castle Hill. The spire of **Matthias church** (Mátyás templom) towers gracefully over the historic district. The church takes its name from Hungary's most popular medieval king who married here twice in the

> Frequent organ and sacred music concerts are held in Matthias church, especially on Friday evenings during summer months.

15th century. The Hapsburg Emperor Franz Joseph I was crowned King of Hungary here in 1867, to the tune of the

Coronation Mass, composed for the occasion by Budapest's favorite son, Franz Liszt (1811–1886).

The original church was constructed in the mid-13th century, converted into a mosque during the Turkish occupation, and seriously damaged during the re-conquest of Buda in 1686. It was rebuilt in baroque style after the return of the Christian forces, and between 1873 and 1896 it was completely reconstructed along its present neo-Gothic lines. The unusual diamond-pattern roof and the geometric designs covering the inside walls date from the 19th-century refurbishment. The interior has attractive stained-glass windows and frescoes by two 19th-century Hungarian artists.

In the **Loreto Chapel** (immediately to the left of the entrance), a red marble statue of the Virgin takes pride of place. Up some stairs entered on the left-hand side of the church are the entrance to the crypt and the **Museum of Ecclesiastical Art.** The museum rambles up and down various old staircases, offering an excellent view, at one spot, down onto the nave. The museum holds a fine collection of medieval stone carvings, historic vestments, religious paintings, and sacred relics, including a replica of the famed **Crown of St. Stephen**. The crown is romantically associated with St. Stephen, the great 11th-century king, but is actually of a slightly later date (the lower half is 11th century; the upper, 12th century). The beautiful goldthreaded mantle, made in 1031, is also said to have belonged to St. Stephen, and is of the right date to have done so (he died in 1038).

In Trinity Square (Szent-háromság tér) in front of the church is the **Holy Trinity column**, crowded with statues of saints and angels, recalling an early 18th-century epidemic of bubonic plague. Survivors built the monument in gratitude for being spared. Across the square, towards Dísz tér,

The medieval spire of Matthias church is echoed by the turrets of the Fishermen's Bastion.

the white two-story baroque building with a jutting corner balcony served as the Buda town hall from 1710 to 1873.

Directly behind Matthias church is one of the most photographed monuments in Budapest, the intriguingly named **Fishermen's Bastion** (Halászbástya), built onto the castle walls. At first glance this picture-book array of turrets, terraces, and arches could easily pass for an authentic medieval fortification, but the bastion was constructed around the turn of the 20th century purely for ornamental reasons. The monument's name is a reference to the fishermen who defended the ramparts here in the 18th century. Today busloads of tourists peer through the arches, enjoying one of the city's finest views — across the Danube and over to the Houses of Parliament. (If you want to walk around on top, you will have to pay; but the views down below are free and pretty much the same.)

Near the handsome equestrian statue of the canonized King István (St. Stephen), the first king of Hungary, old ladies trade Transylvanian tablecloths and street musicians fill the air with the sounds of Bartók and Liszt in return for the dollars, pounds, euros, and yen of tourists.

Just west of Fishermen's Bastion is the jarring façade of the mirrored, six-story Budapest Hilton Hotel. The bold approach of merging ancient and modern has integrated this 1977 Hilton Hotel with the remains of a 17th-century Jesuit college and the tower of a 13th-century Dominican monastery, and the result is certainly not to the liking of all observers. Across Hess András tér, the bas-relief of a red hedgehog at No. 3 recalls the building's days as an inn during the 18th century (the inn was named after the beast in question).

Begin your tour of the district's old streets along delightful **Táncsics Mihály utca**. House No. 7, where Beethoven stayed in 1800, is now the **Museum of the History of Music.** Here you'll learn to distinguish a clavichord from a hurdy-gurdy, and discover that bagpipes originated in Hungary. Next door, at No. 9, are plaques to the political heroes Mihály Táncsics and Lajos Kossuth, both imprisoned here in the 1830s and 1840s for their nationalist beliefs. No. 26 served as a synagogue from the end of the 14th century and has a small museum relating to this period.

The street ends at the **Vienna Gate** (Bécsi kapu), a reminder that the district was once fully enclosed. The grand structure to the left of the gate with the diamond-patterned roof, echoing that of Matthias Church, houses the **National Archives**.

Poet Ferenc Kazinsky is commemorated by this statue outside the National Archive building in the Old Town.

Around the corner is **Fortuna utca**, a charming, much-photographed street full of pastel-painted houses. It takes its name from a tavern that stood at No. 4, from 1785 to 1868. Today it houses the **Museum of Commerce and Catering** (Kereskedelmi és Vendéglátóipari Múzeum) — neither as boring nor as grand as its name would suggest. The exhibits address confectionery in one section and Hungarian trade in the late-19th and early-20th century in another, and the museum curators take a genuine delight in demonstrating various exhibits.

At Szentháromság tér turn back into **Országház utca.** *Országház* means Houses of Parliament, and the street takes its name from the parliamentary sessions that took place in the building at No. 28 between 1790 and 1807. The architectural highlights of the street are the grand 15th-century mansion now occupied by the Alabárdos

The pastel-painted façades lining Fortuna utca make this attractive street a frequent target for photographers.

("Halbadier") restaurant, as well as Nos 18–22, considered three of the finest examples of 14th- and 15th-century domestic architecture on the hill. Several other buildings on this street incorporate picturesque medieval features, at times hidden just inside the archway. Here you'll see ancient stone *sedilia* (built-in seats for three people) and necklaces of paprika strung out to dry across windows and balconies. Though the area is a magnet for visitors, plenty of Budapestis still live here.

At the end of Országház utca rises the ruined **Church of Mary Magdalene,** converted to a mosque under the Turks and reduced to knee-high remains by the Allies in the last days of World War II. Amazingly, its huge 15th-century tower survived. One stone-traceried window was rebuilt, but the rest of the church was left in ruins as a poignant reminder of wartime destruction. A more light-hearted curiosity is visible on the corner of Országház utca and Petermann bíró utca. A "flying nun" in stone (a reference to a convent that occupied No. 28 before the parliament) has apparently passed straight through the corner of the building. Miklós Melocco executed this amusing sculpture in 1977.

Uri utca ("Gentlemen's Street") is even more ancient than Országház utca, and the houses have many fascinating details. Yet another specialist museum crops up at No. 49: the **Telephone Museum** features 110 years of telephone exchanges and technology, and proudly claims that Budapest had the world's first telephone exchange.

At No. 9 you can join a guided tour to descend deep into the hill via a series of tunnels dug in medieval times as an escape route in case of siege. They were used again as air-raid shelters, and as an emergency hospital, in 1944–1945. The caves and tunnels also contain waxworks depicting key episodes from Hungarian history.

Uri utca terminates at Dísz tér, where it is best to turn and walk back along **Tárnok utca.** Among the shops and restaurants here are a number of fine buildings, among them the Aranyhordó ("Golden Barrel") restaurant, with its noteworthy orange and red geometric frescoes painted on the overhanging first floor.

Next door, No. 18 was built as a merchant's house in the first half of the 15th century. From 1750 until 1913, it was the **Golden Eagle Pharmacy** (Arany Sas patikaház). Today it is the most attractive and idiosyncratic of the district's small museums. Beautiful old majolica vessels join informative displays on the curious potions and alchemical practices deployed in the Budapest of this era. Ask one of the guides to point out such curiosities as the 2,000-year-old mummy head, used to provide the "mummy-head dust" prescribed for treating bronchitis.

The last street in this district is the leafy **Tóth Arpád sétány.** This promenade, situated along the western ramparts, offers views of the Buda Hills and of the huge southern railway station (Déli pályaudavar). It is the perfect place for a stroll, particularly in early evening, when Budapestis come out to enjoy the fresh air. At the northern end, various cannons signal the entrance to the **Museum of Military History** (Hadtörténeti Múzeum). The extensive exhibition is popular with school children, and the section dedicated to the 1956 uprising is likely to make the most impact on older visitors.

The Royal Palace

Returned to its former glory after centuries of being razed and rebuilt, the **Royal Palace**, southeast of the Old Town, dominates Castle Hill's southern skyline. Begun in the 13th century as Buda Castle (Budai Vár), the palace reached its

Stepped gardens lead to the ancient Royal Palace, whose mighty bulk crowns the southern edge of Castle Hill.

zenith in the 1400s under King Mátyás, when it was said to be equal in grandeur to that of any castle in Europe. Under the Ottoman Empire it fell into neglect, and during the siege of 1686 it was almost completely demolished.

In the next two centuries the palace was rebuilt in the neo-baroque style. Occupying German forces made the palace their headquarters during their final stand in 1945. Since then, the palace has been rebuilt, not to serve as an official residence or to host government functions, but to house one of Hungary's most important museums.

To approach the Royal Palace from Matthias church, walk along Tárnok utca past Dísz tér. If you are not already on Castle Hill, the best approach to the Royal Palace is from the steps at the southern tip of the hill by the Semmelweis Medical Museum. The path climbs through lovely gardens to the rear entrance of the castle and the only surviving turreted tower, the Buzogány ("Mace") Tower. Steps lead up through tiny castle gardens to the entrance of the **Museum of Budapest History** (Budapesti Történeti Múzeum) in Wing E of the Royal Palace.

It is possible to visit the ten or so rooms that have survived from the original medieval palace of King Mátyás, now faithfully reconstructed. More than four decades of excavations at the palace site have given scholars a good idea of the appearance of the palace. Don't miss the exhibition of the Gothic statues that adorned the medieval building. Thrown out during construction work at the start of the 15th century, they were only rediscovered during excavations in 1974.

The main palace lies through the dramatic black-and-gold courtyard arch. Given its tremendous size, it is difficult to see the entire palace and its multifaceted exhibits in a single day. Give priority to Wings B, C, and D, which house the **Hungarian National Gallery** (Magyar Nemzeti Galéria), a mammoth entity spanning seven centuries of Hungarian art. The gallery has splendid collections of medieval

This splendid baroque gateway leads to the main courtyard of the Royal Palace, which houses artistic treasures from every age.

and Gothic art as well as popular exhibits of Hungarian Impressionism and 20th-century works (in Wings C and D). Several rooms on the first floor of the National Gallery are dedicated to Mihály Munkácsy, a 19th-century painter who became a famous artist in Paris. His dark and gloomy pictures are literally getting darker and gloomier, a result of the bitumen he mixed with his paint. Look out for the works of Hungarian painters László Mednyánszky, József Rippl-Rónai, and Károly Lotz, as well as János Vaszary's pivotal *Golden Age* and the odd but striking works of Tivadar Kosztka Csontváry, on the second floor landing.

Lovers of contemporary art should head for the **Ludwig Collection** in Wing A, the northernmost wing of the palace, which houses works by such important international figures as Andy Warhol, Roy Lichtenstein, and Joseph Beuys.

The southern palace courtyard includes Wing F, which houses the **Széchenyi National Library** and its two million tomes. The library is open to the public, and temporary exhibitions are held in the building.

BUDA RIVERSIDE AND HILLS

Viziváros (Watertown)

The district between Castle Hill and the Danube is called Viziváros, or **Watertown**. In the Middle Ages, the red-roofed district is where commoners lived, beyond the walled area where royalty and wealthier merchants lived on Castle Hill. During the occupation of Buda by the Ottoman Empire, the Turks transformed the area's churches into mosques and built public baths. Today the busy urban area is the site of new hotels, built here to capitalize on the area's proximity to Castle Hill and its unbeatable views of the sprawling Houses of Parliament located directly opposite, across the river.

Golden light filters through tiny windows in the dome of the 16th-century Turkish Király Baths.

The section of riverside lying to the north of the Chain Bridge is an area of wonderful arcades and terraces, adorned with neo-classical statues and ceremonial staircases, as well as gateways (not open to the public) leading up to the Royal Palace. The area can be reached on foot, by walking gently down from Castle Hill, or by taking the metro, bus, tram, or suburban railway to **Batthyány tér**, a major square and city transport hub.

The Vienna stagecoach terminal was once just around the corner from Batthyány tér, and the famous White Cross Inn, on the side of the square opposite the river, was a fashionable venue for balls and other celebrations. It is still a grand old building, even if its role has now been reduced to that of a nightclub, renamed Casanova after the famous Venetian libertine, who is reputed to have stayed here. On the south side of the square is **Szent Anna templom** (St. Anne's Church), a fine mid-18th century structure with Italianate influences and a green steeple.

Farther north along heavily trafficked **Fő utca** is a fine example of a Turkish bath. The **Király Baths** (Király fürdő) were established in the 16th century, and the authentic Turkish section has survived, complete with a large octagonal pool under a dome. In addition to the steam bath, visitors (men on Monday, Wednesday and Friday; women on

Tuesday, Thursday and Saturday) can use the steam sauna and other facilities. (See the box on Budapest's thermal baths on page 78.)

Turn left off Frakel Leó út (the continuation of Fő utca) at Margit híd (Margaret Bridge) and follow the signpost

> At Budapest's thermal baths, a tip (from 200 to 500 Ft) is expected for special services such as massage.

up the steps to another memento of Turkish times, the **Tomb of Gül Baba** (Gül Baba türbe). This meticulously preserved mausoleum and site of Muslim pilgrimage was built in the mid-16th century for Gül Baba, a famous dervish killed during the siege of Buda in 1541. The interior, in keeping with the Muslim tradition, is rather austere; the tomb is surrounded by carpets and a few artworks given by the Turkish government. The hill on which the mausoleum stands, called the Rózsadomb ("Hill of the Roses"), is one of the most exclusive addresses in Budapest.

By contrast with the austerity of the mausoleum, the 1896 neo-Gothic **Calvinist Church** is recognized by its exuberant tile and brick exterior, and is located along the river toward the Chain Bridge, just south of Batthyány tér.

A glorious patchwork of glazed tiles covers the roof of the Calvinist Church.

Gellért Hill

While Castle Hill provides arguably the finest views over the Danube, another lookout point just south of the Royal Palace should not be missed. **Gellért-hegy** (Gellért Hill), which rises some 140 m (460 ft) almost directly above the Danube on the Buda side, affords a wide panorama of the city. It is not well served by public transport, though, and the climb up, starting from the Gellért Hotel, is strenuous.

Almost immediately to the right is an extraordinary monument in the hillside, a cave converted into a chapel. It belongs to the Order of St. Paul, the only monastic body of Hungarian origin. Continue up the slope through the pleasant landscaped gardens of the Jubileumi Park, turn right onto the main road, and you will soon reach the summit.

The **Citadel** crowning the hill was built by the Austrians after the Revolution of 1848 as a lookout point from which to control adjacent Castle Hill. Despised by Hungarians as a symbol of occupation, the Citadel saw no action, however, until the end of World War II, when the German army decamped here. Since then the Citadel has been renovated and now holds a restaurant and café, but it is most often visited for the panoramic views.

The 14-m (46-ft) tall **Liberation Monument** (Szabadsag szobor), visible from all parts of the city, stands below the citadel. The Russians erected it in memory of their troops who fell while "liberating" Budapest from the Germans. The monument is loathed by most locals as a symbol of Soviet domination, but it has become too much of a city landmark to remove.

☛ At the base of the hill, the **Gellért Hotel** is the perfect place to recover from your walk. Behind this classic 1918 art nouveau structure is a huge, landscaped outdoor swimming pool complex (including a pool with a wave machine), while inside (entry on Kelenhegyi út 4) are the finest thermal baths in Buda. The unisex indoor pool has a vaulted glass ceiling and Roman-style carved columns, while the thermal baths (segregated by sex) feature marble statues, fine mosaics and glazed tiles, as well as relaxing waters and such services as mud treatments and Thai massage. The pools and services are open to the public and are a highlight of Budapest for many visitors. (See box on page 78 for additional information about these and other baths.)

Treat yourself to a long and therapeutic soak in the Gellért Hotel, with its majestic pillared and domed swimming pool.

Though the Gellért reigns supreme among Budapest's thermal baths, there are two more historic baths (*fürdő*) along the Buda embankment (*rakpart*), near the Erzsébet híd (Elizabeth Bridge). The entrance to the male-only **Rudas fürdő** is rather shabby, and a few words of bath-related Hungarian are definitely an advantage here, but after more than 400 years of serving the locals, change comes slowly. The building has been much altered over the centuries but not the timeless atmosphere in the steamy main pool, where a stone Turkish dome covers an octagonal pool, and sunlight streams in through the star-shaped glass openings in the cupola. The 16th-century **Rác fürdő**, just south of the entrance to the bridge on the Buda side, is another bath with a Turkish layout. Legend holds that King Mátyás used to visit the baths using secret tunnels connected to the Royal Palace.

On I Apród utca, 1-3, the **Semmelweis Medical History Museum** (Semmelweis Orvostörténeti Múzeum) is named after Professor Semmelweis, who was born here in 1815. By discovering the cause of puerperal fever (which was the main cause of death in childbirth until that time) he became known as the "Mothers' Savior." The museum is a lively — if sometimes gruesome — trawl through old instruments and medical techniques, some of which appear far worse than the condition they were intended to relieve. There is also a beautifully preserved pharmacy shop dating back to 1813.

ÓBUDA & AQUINCUM

Óbuda — literally, "Old Buda" — is the most ancient section of Budapest, being the site of the Roman city of Aquincum,

Modern billboards catch the eye along the road that leads to the ruins of the Roman city of Aquincum.

built in the first century A.D. as the capital of the province of Lower Pannonia. Nowadays it is scarred by heavy traffic using the main northern highway out of the city, and by hurriedly and cheaply built Soviet-style residential buildings. It is in this unlikely setting that Hungary's most impressive Roman ruins are to be found.

To begin the Roman route, take city bus 42 or 106 north along the river on the Buda side, or HÉV train from Batthyány tér to the **Military Amphitheater** (Katonai Amfiteátrum). Gladiators performed here in the second century A.D. to amuse as many as 15,000 legionnaires. Completely forgotten for centuries, the ruins were only partially restored in the 1930s. Now the amphitheater is little more than a grassy piece of parkland where locals walk their dogs, but enough remains of the original walls and outline to give a good idea of what it was once like.

The ruins of the **baths** built for the Roman legions stand further north, beneath the Flórián tér overpass on the Buda side of the Arpád Bridge. Take the walkway on the opposite side from the baths to catch the incongruous sight of a dozen isolated Corinthian columns set against the backdrop of a 1960s housing estate.

The third — and by far most important — Roman site is **Aquincum,** a civilian town constructed for artisans, merchants, priests, and other non-military staff. The ruins can be reached by HÉV train from Batthány tér (20 minutes). The remains of a Roman aqueduct can be seen just before the Aquincum stop, in the central carriageway of the highway which runs close to the railroad track.

The Aquincum site proper covers a large area and comprises the foundations of villas (including some floor mosaics), workshops, and public areas. The ruins of a second amphitheater lie on the other side of the road. You

One of several fine buildings surrounding the colorful Obuda piazza called Fő tér.

will need a little imagination to recreate the scene as it was when 40,000 people lived here nearly 2,000 years ago, but you will find help in the **Aquincum Museum** attached to the site. Here the best of the finds are displayed, including tombstones, statues, some splendid mosaics, and the remains of a water organ.

There is more to Óbuda than just its Roman heritage. Between Flórián tér and the river is the old town square, called **Fő tér,** a small, picturesque and handsomely renovated piazza untouched by modern development. In this oasis you will find a fine old theater, several pleasant cafés, four first-class restaurants and two excellent museum-galleries.

The first is in the Zichy Palace, the handsome baroque building that dominates the square, now home to the **Vasarely Museum**. This features work by the artist Victor Vasarely, the internationally renowned pioneer of the Op Art movement, which exploits optical effects, characterized by cubes and spheres in bright, eye-popping colors.

Standing by the square near the **Imre Varga Museum** (at Laktanya utca 7) are charming figures with umbrellas, a clue to the collection inside. Varga is renowned as Hungary's greatest living sculptor. Whether his materials and subject matter are conventional (as in the case of *Umbrellas*) or more offbeat (as with many of his works) he always manages to remain accessible and popular.

Buda Hills

The Buda Hills make up an area of greenbelt due west of Rózsadomb, stretching as far north as Óbuda and as far south as the start of the M7 highway. On a clear day, catch any one of the several trams or buses that go to the cog-railway terminus (just west of Moszkva tér, opposite the Hotel Budapest). There is room on the cog-train for mountain bikes if you are feeling particularly active.

The train passes smart residential houses on its way to the terminus and park of Sváb-hegy. A short walk across the park (just follow the crowds) is another railway — this time the **Children's Railway** (Széchenyi-hegyi Gyermekvasút), so named because it is operated almost entirely by school-children (the only adults are the engine drivers).

The old narrow-gauge line climbs slowly, ever-upwards, through unspoiled forests crossed by numerous walking trails. There is a ski-run at the first stop, Normafa, but stay on the train until János-hegy. From here it is a 15-minute walk to the **János-hegy lookout tower**, the highest point in the city at 529 m (1,735 ft). If the horizon is not blurred by haze, there's a great 360-degree view. You can also eat in the lookout café.

If you would like to return to town by a different route, there is a chairlift (closed some Mondays) less than a kilometer (half a mile) west of the János-hegy station. This descends to a camping site, from where you catch the 158 bus (to Moszkva tér). As you float peacefully down the mountainside, you will enjoy some spectacular views over forests to the spires and rooftops of the city.

CROSSING THE DANUBE

Just as Tower Bridge is the epitome of London, Brooklyn Bridge the symbol of New York, and the Golden Gate the pride of San Francisco, so Budapest also has its landmark river crossings.

The most venerable of these is the **Chain Bridge** (Széchenyi Lánchíd). Inaugurated in 1849, it was the first to link Buda and Pest. Count István Széchenyi, a great innovator of his age, imported the technology and expertise of Britain's Industrial Revolution to help Hungary's own reform program. An English engineer, William Tierney Clark, designed the bridge, and its construction was supervised by a Scotsman, Adam Clark (no relation), after whom the square is named at the Buda end of the

bridge. The Chain Bridge has graceful twin arches and is guarded by a pair of massive stone lions at each approach. Don't miss the floodlit bridge at night — it is one of the city's finest sights. (Traditional children's stories maintain that the bridge sneaks into the nearby tunnel to sleep at night, but all that really

Lions guard the approach to the symbolic Chain Bridge, a masterpiece of 19th-century engineering.

happens is that the lights are turned off promptly at midnight.)

South of the Chain Bridge is the rather more functional-looking **Elizabeth Bridge** (Erzsébet híd), named after the consort of Franz Joseph, who was tragically assassinated in 1898. The original bridge was destroyed during World War II. The replacement, which opened in 1964, is of modern design, and works on the suspension principle. Farther south from Elizabeth Bridge is the green iron-built **Liberty Bridge** (Szabadság híd), which dates to 1896 and was originally called the Franz Joseph Bridge. Look for the turul birds perched on a golden ball balancing on each pillar.

To the north of the Chain Bridge is **Margaret Bridge** (Margit híd), a modern replacement of the 19th-century version destroyed in World War II. There are fine stone carvings of nymphs, resembling ship's figureheads, on the bridge piers.

PEST

Modern Budapest lies east of the Danube in what was, until 1873, the autonomous city of Pest. With its conglomeration of hotels, museums, government offices, banks, shopping streets, nightclubs, cafés, busy boulevards and handsome art nouveau apartment buildings, Pest is where the pulse of the modern capital beats strongest.

The Inner City (Belváros)

In A.D. 294 the Romans built a fortress on the great expanse of flat plains to the east of the river to make it harder for invaders to establish a foothold near their garrison. They called the place Contra-Aquincum; today it is the core of the Inner City (Belváros), the glitziest and most fashionable district of Budapest.

The focal point of Pest's pedestrian zone is **Váci utca** (pronounced "*Vah-tsee oot-sa*"), the first place to visit for shopping in the city. Here you will find the best in international fashion, art, cosmetics, books, and jewelry, as well as the Pest Színház (theater) where Franz Liszt made his city début as a 12-year-old pianist. Budapestis — joined by foreign visitors to the city — parade up and down this street every evening.

Váci utca empties north into the shopping square called **Vörösmarty tér**, lined with craft stalls and one of Pest's best gathering places. A classic rest stop for locals and visitors alike is **Gerbeaud**,

Take your pick from tables on the sunny outdoor terrace or high-ceilinged rooms inside at the Gerbeaud café.

doyen of Budapest's café scene since 1884. If the sumptuous, high-ceilinged interior is a little too formal for your liking, then take a terrace seat and watch the world go by.

Stroll a few yards towards the river and you will come to **Vigadó tér**, a pleasant riverside square with unequalled views of Castle Hill. Here, too, you will find craft stalls, and any number of buskers. A vibrant café-restaurant fills one side of the square, but the dominant building is the **Pesti Vigadó theater**. The acoustically perfect auditorium was renovated in 1980 (its predecessors having twice perished in war and revolution), but the glorious mid-19th century Hungarian-Eastern style façade has survived. The list of performers and conductors who have graced the Vigadó theater is a Who's Who of the past 150 years of European classical music: Liszt, Brahms, Wagner, Mahler, Bartók, Prokofiev, Casals, Björling, and von Karajan among them.

From Vörösmarty tér, take Deák Ferenc utca to busy Deák tér. Deák tér is the only point where all three metro lines meet, so it is an apt place for the tiny **Metro Museum** (FAV Múzeum), located down in the pedestrian subway. Here you can see the original train that traveled on Europe's first continental underground railway in 1896.

Nearby is the **National Lutheran Museum**, charting the history of Protestantism in this largely Catholic country, and almost opposite, next door to McDonald's, is a helpful **Tourinform** tourist information office. The mustard-colored building dominating the far side of the square is the **Anker Palace**, formerly an insurance company headquarters, and one of the few structures to escape World War II unscathed.

Walk down Barczy utca, which runs along the back of the Lutheran Church and, on your right, the **Budapest City Hall** fills an entire street. It was built in 1711 as a home for disabled soldiers, served for a time as an army barracks, and became the town hall in 1894. The 19th-century neo-classical Pest County Hall lies a little farther beyond the bend in the same street.

Near here is Szervita tér, notable for a splendid patriotic-religious mosaic, in art nouveau style, on the gable of the old **Turkish Banking House** (Török Bánkház). Head south along Petofi Sándor utca; on your right is the **Paris Arcade** (Párisi Udvar), built in 1909. Inside, look up to enjoy the exotic art nouveau styling and glasswork. At the front is a tourist information office.

Three fine churches, and part of the university complex, lie directly across the busy road (it is best to use the underpass to reach them). The **Franciscan Church**, constructed around 1758, stands on the corner of Ferenciek tere. The relief on the sidewall depicts the flood of 1838, which caused massive destruction in the entire inner city. Continue along Károlyi Mihály utca, past the yellow University Library building on your left. On the opposite corner is the **University Church** (Egyetemi templom). Built between 1725 and 1742 by the monks of the Order of St. Paul, it features rich baroque carving. There are more university buildings on the quiet street called Szerb utca, as well as the **Serbian Church**, which dates from 1688 and has a beautiful interior.

Kossuth Lajos turns into Szabadsajtó út as it approaches the river. On the right-hand side, along Március ter 15, is the oldest building in Pest, the **Inner City Parish Church**

(Belvárosi templom), now hemmed into an undignified position by the Elizabeth Bridge. The soot-covered baroque exterior is rather unremarkable, but the handsome interior conceals much more interesting elements. Founded in the 12th century, some Romanesque construction is still visible. So, too, is the influence of the Turks,

The churches and libraries of Budapest's University Square form a fine architectural ensemble.

who turned the church into a mosque and carved a *mihrab* (prayer niche) on the Mecca side of the chancel wall. Next to the church is all that remains of the ancient Roman defenses of Contra-Aquincum — an excavated square with benches and a small display of tablets and reliefs found on the site.

The Little Boulevard

A medieval town grew around this old Roman defense post, evolving into a long, narrow strip boxed in by the Danube to the west and defensive walls on the other sides. The so-called Kis-körút (Little Boulevard) follows the line of the old walls and encloses the district of Belváros. Despite its name, the Little Boulevard is very big on traffic; it is definitely not the place for a leisurely stroll. There are, however, three major points of interest that fall just outside the inner city side along this notional dividing line.

The Budapest **Central Market Hall** (Vásárcsarnok) is at the beginning of Vámház körút, by the Szabadság híd (Liberty Bridge). This vast and old-fashioned covered market teems with local color and exotic smells. There is also a lively daily market at Lehel tér, north of the inner city in the Lipótváros district (take metro line 3 to the station at Lehel tér).

The **Hungarian National Museum** (Magyar Nemzeti Múzeum) was Hungary's first public collection and it remains the country's largest museum. The impressive structure, built in 1846 in neo-classical style with Corinthian columns and a sculptured tympanum, stands back off the road in its own garden. Inside, amid monumental architectural and ornamental details, the whole story of Hungary unfolds — from the history of the Carpathian Basin from prehistoric times right up to the

21st century. On display are prehistoric remains and ancient jewels and tools, Roman mosaics, a 17th-century Turkish tent fitted out with grand carpets, a baroque library, and royal regalia. The museum used to hold the Holy Crown and Crown Jewels of Hungary but these have been moved to the Houses of Parliament and may yet move again to a permanent home, most likely in Buda.

> **Concerts are frequently held in the Great Synagogue, accompanied by the unusual and massive 1859 organ.**

Back on the Little Boulevard, at the start of Dohány utca, is a striking synagogue of enormous proportions, built in a flamboyant Byzantine-Moorish style. The **Great Synagogue** (Nagy Zsinagóga) dates from the mid-19th century, and is marked by two onion-shaped copper domes. Claimed as the largest synagogue in Europe (and the second largest in the world, behind New York), it is capable of holding up to 3,000 people. The synagogue has been meticulously reno-vated with the assistance of international Jewish foundations.

In an annex, an interesting **Jewish Museum** contains a moving exhibition concerned with the Hungarian Holocaust. Next door to the museum, in a courtyard of the synagogue, is a metal weeping willow, fashioned by the artist Imre Varga (see page 42).

Moorish arabesques and floral patterns decorate the dome of the Great Synagogue.

Each leaf bears the name of one of the Budapest families that perished in the Holocaust. The site was deliberately chosen because it lies above the mass graves of Jews executed by the fascist Arrow Cross government installed by the Nazis between 1944 and 1945. The founder of Modern Zionism, Theodore Herzl (1860–1904) was born in a house on the site where the museum now stands.

Leopold Town (Lipótváros)

Bounded by Jozséf Attila utca to the south and by Bajcsy-Zsilinszky út to the east, Leopold Town (Lipótváros) lies just north of the inner city. Directly opposite the approach to the Chain Bridge is Roosevelt tér, a

Embroidered and handspun blouses are part of the city's folk-art tradition.

square named after the US president. Gresham Palace, the grand art-nouveau building facing the square, was built in 1907 and is being converted to a new luxury hotel. The statue in the middle of the square is of Ferenc Deák, a 19th-century Hungarian who brokered the Austria-Hungary Compromise establishing a dual monarchy (see page 19).

Directions to find the **Basilica of St. Stephen** (Szent István Bazilika) — three blocks east of Roosevelt Square — are hardly needed, as its 96-m (315-ft) dome dominates the skyline. Finished in 1905, after half a century of work, the largest church in Budapest can hold 8,500 people, and is often full to capacity. The exterior is undergoing slow restoration. Before going inside, take the long walk up to the top of the dome for Pest's highest viewpoint (exactly equal in height to the dome of the Houses of Parliament). The macabre main attraction is held in a reliquary in a rear chapel: Szent Jobb (literally "Holy Right") is the much-revered right hand of St. Stephen.

Szabadság tér (Independence Square), a short walk to the north, is probably Pest's finest architectural ensemble. At its center is an obelisk dedicated to the Soviet troops who fell in the city, but the large, showy buildings surrounding the square are what really steal the show. The superb lemon-colored art nouveau building at No. 12 is home to the American Embassy. South of the embassy is the **Hungarian National Bank** and former **Postal Savings Bank** building, a lovely example of Secessionist, or art nouveau, architecture, built in 1901 and ornamented with glazed ceramic tiles and floral mosaics. Across the square is the former Stock Exchange (now the country's TV headquarters — called MTV but wholly unrelated to the airing of music videos), an eclectic-style building designed by the same architect as the Hungarian National Bank. In the movie version of *Evita*, it served as the Argentine presidential building, or Casa Rosada. Have a look at the interesting reliefs on all of these buildings.

The great dome of the **Houses of Parliament** (Országház), where the national government holds its sessions, is clearly visible from the square. The Parliament was built between 1885 and 1904 to symbolize the grandeur of the Austro-Hungarian empire. At its completion it was the largest parliament building in the world: 268 m (879 ft) long, 691 rooms, and with an estimated 20 km (12 miles) of staircase inside. The architect may not have had London's Houses of Parliament in mind, but the neo-Gothic arches and turrets rarely escape comparison with those of Westminster.

Visitors are admitted on guided tours, and only to certain parts of the building, when parliament is not in session. Tours begin to the right of the main stairs and enter through the grandiose central stairway to a splendid 16-sided domed hall, then into the lobby, and finally into the principal debating chamber of the House. Look for the brass rack where deputies leave their cigars before they enter the chamber.

Across from the Houses of Parliament is the mighty **Ethnographic Museum** (Néprazji Múzeum), built in 1893

The Crown Jewels

The Hungarian royal regalia — for the most part much older even than the British Crown Jewels — have endured a long and turbulent history of disappearance and recovery. In 1464 the crown — the symbol of the Hungarian nation — was stolen from the country, and King Mátyás had to ransom it back again. A maid from the Citadel of Visegrád stole the crown and jewels again in the 16th century.

In later centuries the regalia were buried in Transylvania (then part of Hungary) to keep them from the Hapsburgs. At the end of World War II the Soviets carried it to Austria, and then Americans got hold of it and kept it in Fort Knox, safe from the clutches of the Communists, until 1978. The jewels were then returned to Hungary, where they still reside — though they have moved from the Hungarian National Museum to the Houses of Parliament, and there is talk now of relocating them permanently to the Palace on Castle Hill. The last king to actually wear the Holy Crown associated with St. Stephen was the Hapsburg monarch Károly IV, in 1916.

to house the Supreme Court of Justice. It is worth a visit for the palatial interiors alone, but the exhibits of Hungarian folk art, typical Hungarian dress and Hungarian rural life are also quite interesting. Just south of the museum in a quiet plaza is a recently unveiled **sculpture of Imre Nagy** standing in overcoat and hat on a bridge. Nagy was the Communist head turned reformer who was executed by the Soviets for his part in the 1956 Uprising.

☞ Andrássy út

The most attractive avenue in the city, modeled on the Champs-Elysées in Paris, was driven through the city straight as an arrow for almost 2.4 km (1 mile) in the 1870s. Connecting the inner city to City Park, it is lined by some of Budapest's finest architecture. Nearly every building has some unique feature — a fountain or statue, a mosaic, frieze, column or arcade. The elegance of the leafy avenue belies the prosaic nature of its former names — it has been known

variously as Népköztársaság útja (People's Republic Avenue), Sugár út (Radial Road) and even — to the disgust of Budapestis — as Stalin út.

You can visit one of the typically large *fin-de-siècle* aristocratic homes right at the beginning of the avenue, at No.

A statue of political reformer Imre Nagy gazes towards the Houses of Parliament.

3, now home to the **Postal Museum**. It maintains some colorful and interesting exhibits (such as correspondence between Thomas Edison and the Hungarian telecommunications pioneer Tivadar Puskás), but the real attraction is the building itself, particularly the stairway and balcony decorated with outstanding frescoes by Károly Lotz.

Farther up the avenue, at No. 222, is the neo-Renaissance **Hungarian State Opera House**, completed in 1884 by Miklós Ybl and the most admired building on the avenue. Its Italianate style and restrained proportions fit in exquisitely with its surroundings. The splendidly opulent gilt and marble interior may be visited on hour-long guided tours (conducted daily at 3pm

Budapest's favorite composer, Frans Liszt, is portrayed in bronze.

and 4pm in several languages, subject to performances). Its architecture, atmosphere, and acoustics rank among the very best in Europe. If you are an opera lover, you will certainly enjoy the performances here.

Dreschler House, the art nouveau building across the street, was once home to the State Ballet. Down the small street to the right is the **New Theater**, topped by a colorful piece of geometric art nouveau embellishment.

The pedestrian-only block called **Liszt Ferenc tér** holds a number of theaters, restaurants and chic cafés. In the middle stands an excellent modern statue of Liszt — portrayed conducting in a caricature of flailing hands and windswept hair. The **Academy of Music**, completed in

Young skateboarders treat Heroes' Square as one big adventure playground.

1907, is found at the end of the street. This art nouveau gem has a handsome façade, lobby, and interior. It is quite easy to get a look inside when a concert isn't scheduled; alternatively, try to attend a performance here.

Cross the busy intersection of Oktogon, and three streets north at Vörösmarty utca 35 you will find the **Franz Liszt Memorial Museum**. This delightful small collection of pianos, memorabilia, and period furnishings is set in an apartment where the composer once lived (closed Sunday and the first three weeks of August).

As Andrássy út edges closer to City Park, the villas get noticeably grander and mansions in garden settings predominate. Many are now home to embassies. The square called **Kodály körönd** (named after another Hungarian composer, Zoltán Kodály) is a splendid ensemble, its curving façades decorated with classical figures and inlaid motifs.

At No. 103 is another charming small collection in the **Museum of East Asian Art** (Hopp Ferenc Kelet-ázsiai Múzeum), which rotates pieces from Ferenc Hopp's collection comprising 20,000 exotic items. A related **Museum of Chinese Art** (Kína Múzeum), also known as the György Ráth Múzeum, lies south of here, occupying a handsome art nouveau villa at Városligeti fasor 12.

Andrássy út ends in a burst of pomp at **Heroes' Square** (Hősök tere), a huge open square housing the **Millennium**

Monument, built on the 1,000th anniversary of the Magyar settlement of the region. The 36-m (118-ft) column supports the figure of the Archangel Gabriel who, according to legend, appeared to St. Stephen in a dream and offered him the crown of Hungary. Around the pedestal sit Prince Arpád and the Magyar tribal chiefs on horseback, while flanking the column is a semi-circular colonnade with statues of historical figures, starting with King Stephen. In front of the statuary is the Tomb of the Unknown Soldier. The deadly serious Communist demonstrations of yesteryear that took place here have given way to youthful skateboarders who hang out at the base of the Millennium Monument and bob and weave through cones set up around the square.

Facing each other across Heroes' Square are two large neo-classical structures that are near mirror images of each other — not surprising, since they are by the same architect. On the left is the **Museum of Fine Arts** (Szépművészeti Múzeum), holding the city's most highly regarded and wide-ranging collection, including Egyptian mummies, Greek and Roman relics (the latter collection is undergoing long-term restoration), Renaissance works, and about 2,500 Old Masters, of which some 800 are on show at any one time. Italian, Dutch, German, and Spanish schools are all superbly represented. The latter is particularly notable, constituting one of the best collections of Spanish Old Masters outside Spain, with masterpieces by El Greco, Goya, and others. There are also rooms dedicated to English, French, and Flemish artists. A favorite of many visitors is the 19th-century collection, including a treasure trove of French Impressionist and Post-Impressionist artists such as Cézanne, Pisarro, Monet, Gauguin, and Renoir. Leonardo da Vinci is featured in sculpture and prints and drawings sections. (In 2001 the museum was undergoing extensive renovation, which relegated the collection of Old Masters on the first floor to galleries half the size of the space habitually dedicated to them.)

Opposite the Museum of Fine Arts is the **Mucsarnok**, or Palace of Art, which mounts high-quality temporary exhibitions of contemporary Hungarian and foreign artists. Reopened in 1995 after renovation, the gallery boasts the finest art bookstore in Budapest, not to mention a beautiful exterior, crowned by a splendid pediment mosaic of St. Stephen in his role as patron saint of the arts. There is also a smaller sister branch in the City Park (directions are posted on the front of the Mucsarnok).

☛ City Park (Városliget)

In addition to its role as a memorial to Hungarian history, Heroes' Square serves as a gateway to the large expanse known as City Park, a lovely green space where Budapestis relax, stroll, picnic, hire row boats, go to the zoo, and visit museums. The park, which covers some 101 hectares (250 acres), began to evolve in the early 19th century, though many of the present amenities were added during preparations for the Magyar Millennium festivities of 1896.

Cross the bridge over the boating lake, which doubles as an ice-skating rink in winter. The **Castle of Vajdahunyad**, behind the lake, was built as a prop for the Millennium Exhibition in 1896 but proved so popular that it was rebuilt in permanent form. It reproduces in convincing detail part of the exterior of the fairytale Hunyadi castle in Transylvania. Inside the castle is the **Museum of Hungarian Agriculture**, housing a comprehensive collection that illustrates the history of hunting, fishing, and farming. If you want to see the castle at its best, return by night, when it is beautifully illuminated.

Within the grounds, there is a **Catholic church** (Ják Chapel) with a Romanesque portal (another reconstruction) and one of the city's favorite statues. It is called *Anonymous* and it depicts the medieval chronicler who gave Hungary its first written records. The scribe's face is hidden deep inside the cowl of his monkish robe; aspiring writers seek inspiration by touching his pen.

The Moorish-style Elephant House stands in the City Zoo.

The jewel in the park is the **Széchenyi Baths** complex, to the left of the road that bisects the park. One of the largest medicinal bath complexes in Europe, it provides year-round, open-air swimming, at a constant temperature of 27°C (81°F), in beautiful surroundings. The neo-baroque buildings, bright yellow and topped by a series of huge green domes, opened in 1881. Inside the pool area, surrounded by ivy-clad walls, and sumptuous statuary, groups of men stand up to their chests in warm water amidst the steam, concentrating intently on games of chess (the chess boards form part of the small jetties that protrude into the pool).

Just behind the baths are the zoo and two amusement parks. The **City Zoo**, one of the oldest in the world (1866), welcomes visitors with an art nouveau entrance decorated with polar bears and elephants. The recently restored Elephant House is a handsome Oriental-Hungarian construction with a tall minaret. Renovations on several pavilions have produced more free-roaming grounds. The Palm House, the largest tropical hall in Central Europe, reopened at the end of 2000. Next to the zoo is Gundel, an upper crust restaurant that is legendary in Hungarian culinary circles.

Vidám Park, next door, is an old-fashioned, funfair-style amusement park for the kids. You won't find American-style thrill rides here, just low-tech carousels, bumper cars, and a Ferris wheel. Adjoining it is a mini-version of the park, more suited to younger children. Next door to the amusement parks, a circus makes regular appearances throughout the year.

Another enjoyable family attraction is the **Transport Museum** in the southeastern corner of the park, unmistakably signaled by the vintage train that appears to be roaring right out of the building. Inside you'll find vintage locomotives, motorcycles and antique horse-drawn carriages.

Architecture buffs should keep their eyes peeled for splendid examples of art nouveau architecture (or Secessionism, as the early 20th-century style was known in Hungary) near City Park. One unusually shaped building is home to the **National Association for the Blind** (Hermina utca 47). Another, slightly more out of the way, is the **Geology Institute** (Stefánia út 14), a fantastic structure topped by blue tiles and statues of Atlases (male figures supporting globes) that would not look out of place in Antoni Gaudí's Barcelona. Try to see the lobby if it is open. Another terrific example of the style is the **Egger Villa** (Városligeti fasor 24).

The Great Boulevard (Nagy-körút)

The big and bustling Great Boulevard (Nagy-körút) forms a long, sweeping arc from Margaret Bridge to the Petofi Bridge. City planners approved the project and pushed it through during the landmark Magyar Millennium year of 1896, when the volume of traffic was considerably less than it is today.

The architectural pride of the Great Boulevard is without doubt the **Museum of Applied Arts** (Iparm u vészeti Múzeum), just off Ferenc körút at Nos 33-37 Ülloi út. The splendid art nouveau exterior incorporates Hungarian folk art and majolica tiles. Great green oriental cupolas, small spiky towers, a majolica lantern, and a bright green and gold tiled roof crown the edifice. The museum's architect, Ödön Lechner (who also built the distinguished Postal Savings Bank in Leopold Town), is regarded as the greatest exponent of this native form of art nouveau style (called Secessionism). The interior is just as remarkable: Hungarian with strong (and fantastical) Moorish influences. Shimmering white arches, balconies, and swirling staircases

Fittingly, the Museum of Applied Arts is itself a fine example of folk art and decorative art-nouveau tilework.

sweep up to a fine art nouveau skylight. The main hall is covered by a great expanse of glass supported by an iron frame, and ferns and potted plants around the hall create a winter garden ambience.

A fascinating permanent exhibition, showing the progress of native arts and crafts techniques from the 12th century onwards, is augmented by a variety of temporary exhibitions, which are usually of a very high quality, on more specialized subjects. The section on art nouveau from around the world is particularly attractive and instructive.

A museum of a much more restrained nature lies just beyond Erzsébet körút, at Hársfa utca 47. The **Philatelic Museum** (Bélyeg Múzeum) contains every stamp issued by Hungary from 1871 onwards, and provides pictorial history of the country in miniature.

Teréz körút and Erzsébet körút have traditionally been centers of Budapest's cultural, as well as its commercial, life. At the Great Boulevard's intersection with Dohány utca is the **New York Café** (formerly known as the Hungaria). The café's neo-baroque and art nouveau interior, shining with polished wood, brass, and cut glass, has been restored to its original gaudy glory, so that it looks the same as it did at the beginning of the 20th century. The exterior is covered in scaffolding — and has been for about as long as anyone can remember.

Margaret Island (Margit-sziget)

The elite of the Roman Empire used to escape to this leafy oasis between the two banks of the Danube, and later princes and plutocrats followed in their footsteps. Today tourists enjoy the thermal facilities and treatments offered at two hotels on the island, while Budapestis come to walk, bike, play tennis and enjoy picnics on sunny afternoons. The leisure establishment most of interest to visitors is the huge outdoor Palatinus Baths (Palatinus strand) complex, with its thermal pools and wave pool, capable of accommodating an astonishing 20,000 swimmers and sunbathers.

Margaret Island is 2 km (1¼ miles) long and only a few hundred yards at the widest. Many of its population of 10,000 trees are now more than a century old, and large areas of the island have been landscaped. Best of all, cars (with a few exceptions) are prohibited, thus preserving the island's peace and quiet.

People (and Hungarian Vizsla dogs) come to relax in the sunshine on Margaret Island.

Alongside a landmark octagonal water tower is an open-air theater, which presents concerts, opera, and ballet performances in the summer. Nearby are the ruins of a 13th-century **Dominican Convent** founded by King Béla IV. The king enrolled his 11-year-old daughter, Margit, at the convent in fulfillment of a vow he had made should he live to survive the Mongol invasion. Princess (and later Saint) Margit remained on the island for the rest of her life. A marble plaque marks her burial place.

Other ruins close by include those of a **Franciscan Church** and monastery built in the 13th century. The charming little **Premonstratensian Chapel** — a 20th-century reconstruction of the original 12th-century church — is still in use today. It houses a 15th-century bell, the oldest in Hungary.

The Outskirts of Budapest

Two relatively recent additions of relatively specialized interest have been built on the outskirts of the capital.

Statue Park (Szoborpark Múzeum; open daily 10am–dusk; 1 December–28 February, weekends only) is a slightly surreal open-air theme park (or graveyard, perhaps) used to display some 30 or so monumental statues once imposed by the Communist regime on the streets of Budapest. Rather than see them destroyed by enraged citizens — the fate of many such examples of state art in other Central European countries — the Budapest authorities have preserved them for posterity in this suburban park. Giant socialist-realist figures of Lenin and worker heroes strut against the backdrop of newly built homes. Getting there is a little complicated. Szobor Park lies in the XXIII district on the corner of Balatoni út and Szabadkai út, about 45 minutes by bus from the city center. Take bus 50 or 7-173 to Etele tér terminus and then yellow Volán bus from stall 2 or 3 toward Diósd (a taxi is much simpler but more expensive, of course).

Once ubiquitous, Lenin now has to be sought out in Statue Park.

Train aficionados will adore a brand-new addition to the city's landscape, the **Rail Heritage Park** (Magyar Vasúttörténeti Park; Tel. 428-0180; <www.mavnosz talgia.hu>), designed as an interactive train park. The park is about 15 minutes from downtown Budapest, and has about 70 vintage steam locomotives and coaches for kids of all ages to play on, including unique rotating loading docks. To get there, take the shuttle train called the *különvonat* from the Nyugati Train Station.

DAY TRIPS FROM BUDAPEST

A short distance north of Budapest, the Danube dramatically alters its easterly course for a southern tack. The prosaic name of this extraordinary region is Dunakanyar, meaning the Danube Bend. Here the river is at its most alluring, the countryside lush and unspoiled, and there are three delightful historic towns to explore, all within easy reach of Budapest.

Szentendre

Only 20 km (12 miles) from central Budapest is Szentendre (*"sen-ten-druh"*), perhaps the most captivating of the Danube Bend settlements. The picturesque town is known for its artists' colony and a surprising number of small museums and galleries (close to 100 in total). The easiest way to reach the town is by HÉV suburban railway from Batthyány tér in Buda (about 45 minutes). During summer, boats make a five-hour journey all the way from Budapest to Esztergom, stopping en route at Szentendre and Visegrád.

Though the approach to Szentendre is lined by expanding modern suburbs — increasingly, people are choosing to live here and commute to Budapest — the heart of the town remains virtually locked in the 18th century. Serbian refugees twice settled here in the wake of Turkish invasions: first in the late 13th century, and then again in 1690. On the latter occasion, around 8,000 Serbs brought their religion, art, architecture, and commercial acumen to Szentendre.

The majestic Serbian church on the hill is the town's most prominent landmark. Right at the center of town is **Fő tér**, a picture-postcard square lined with 18th- and 19th-century houses that once belonged to wealthy burghers. The Serbian community erected the iron rococo memorial cross in the center of the plaza in 1763, in gratitude for being spared by the plague. The small church in the square, the Blagovestenska Eastern Orthodox Church, is better known as the **Greek Church** (because of the Greek Orthodox rites practiced within) even though it, too, is Serbian. Built in the mid-18th century, its interior is a gem, with a collection of Serb-painted icons well worth seeing.

Facing the church, on the left-hand side, in what used to be an 18th-century schoolhouse, is the **Ferenczy Museum**, displaying works by the Hungarian Impressionist Károly Ferenczy and his two offspring. Another museum is on the opposite side of the church, the **Margit Kovács Museum**,

Fő tér, with its plague memorial cross and patrician houses, marks the centre of picturesque Szentendre.

the former home and workshop of the ceramicist Margit Kovács (1907–1977), unknown outside Hungary but worthy of an international audience. Inside are several rooms of her very personal sculptures of wide-eyed damsels, poignant religious icons, and ordinary people captured in tragic poses.

The rust-red, mid-18th century **Serbian Orthodox Church** perched on the hill is only open for services, but within its grounds is the excellent **Collection of Serbian Ecclesiastical Art**, displaying precious carvings, icons, and manuscripts. The oldest church in the town lies just above here on top of the hill, affording a perfect vantage point from which to peer down into the tiny gardens and courtyards and across the town's venerable rooftops.

The **Catholic parish church** dates mostly from the 13th century, though parts of it go back to the 11th century. During summer and early autumn, craft and souvenir stalls congregate around here. Opposite the church is another good collection of work by a local artist, that of the Impressionist **Béla Czóbel**. Among the many other art collections on display in the town, don't miss the modern art in the **Barcsay Collection** (on the road out to the bus and railway station).

If you want a change from museums and galleries, a 4-km (2-mile) trip out of town brings you to the **Hungarian Open Air Village Museum** (Sza-badtéri Néprajzi Múzeum) (note that the village is closed from November to April). Catch the No. 8 bus departing from the terminal next to the HÉV station, and ask for the "Skanzen". There are also regular buses from the Tourinform office, on the road from the bus station to the center of Szentendre.

The 46-hectare (115-acre) museum site contains several "villages" of real houses, churches, mills, farm buildings, workshops, and smithies, dating mostly from the late-18th to the early 20th centuries, and gathered

The Skansen Open Air Village is a timeless slice of rural Hungary.

from all over Hungary. Live demonstrations give a fascinating and picturesque simulation of rural Hungary, brought to life by active craftspeople, gingerbread makers, and the like. Don't miss the opportunity to climb up the hill to visit the **Greek Catholic Church** from Mándok (in northeast Hungary), originally built in 1670, which has a fine painted iconostasis.

Visegrád

The next stop along the river, where the Danube truly bends, is Visegrád (*"vee-shuh-grod"*), accessible by boat or bus from Szentendre. The town is situated on one of the most picturesque sections of the river, where verdant hills roll down almost to the water's edge. The finest place to enjoy the views — reminiscent of the best of the Rhine — are from the Citadel, high on a hill above the ruins of the old palace of Visegrád (which means "High Castle" in Slavic).

The strategic value of a site commanding the river bend was appreciated as early as the fourth century, when the Romans built a fort here. In the 14th century, the Angevin kings of Hungary built a **palace** on the site, each monarch adding new rooms and piling on opulence until the building covered an area now estimated at some 18 hectares (45 acres). Sigismund was crowned King of

Hungary and Holy Roman Emperor at the castle in 1403. By the end of the 15th century, when King Mátyás (see page 16) resided here, the palace was famous throughout Europe as an "earthly paradise." One notorious resident was the monstrous Vlad the Impaler (on whom the Dracula legend was partly based), held prisoner here from 1462 to 1475.

Like the Royal Palace in Buda, the palace of Visegrád fell into ruin during the Turkish occupation (though it was not captured and destroyed by the Turks) and was eventually forgotten. Excavations began in 1930; part of the main building has been unearthed and certain parts have been rebuilt (using obviously new materials to differentiate these sections from the original ones). Among the best of the discoveries are the superb Hercules Fountain (a rare vestige of Hungarian Renaissance architecture), the vaulted galleries of the Court of Honor, and the restored Lion's Fountain. On the hillside, the hexagonal tower is known as the Tower of Solomon.

Topping it all is the **Citadel**, once considered so impregnable that the Hungarian crown jewels were kept here. A small museum inside the citadel will either strike children as ghoulish or fascinating: it has life-size representations of medieval executions, including beheading and burning-at-the-stake.

Rescued from ruin: Visegrád's ancient Citadel stands high on a hill above the wooded banks of the Danube.

Esztergom

The last of the important Danube-Bend towns, Esztergom ("*ess-tair-gohm*"), is situated another 20 km (12 miles) upriver. It is linked by hydrofoil to Budapest, and by boat or bus to Szentendre and Visegrád. Take the boat if you have a couple hours to spare, as the river's most scenic stretch lies between Visegrád and Esztergom.

King Stephen was born in Esztergom, which during his lifetime was the capital of Hungary. The town remains the religious center of the country and has the largest church in the land. The towering **Basilica** stands on the site of an 11th-century church where Stephen was crowned the first king of Hungary in the year 1000. That church was destroyed in battle against the Turks. For all its massive dimensions the only part of the current structure that generates an ancient atmosphere is the rather spooky crypt.

The most valuable part of the basilica is the red-marble side chapel called the **Bakócz-kápolna** — a pure example of Italian Renaissance style. Constructed in the 16th century, the chapel, salvaged from the ruins around it and reassembled in the 19th century, is all that survives of the original basilica. A highlight of the basilica is the **treasury** (closed from November to April, as is the tower). This contains Hungary's richest collec-

The Basilica at Esztergom, the medieval capital of all Hungary, is the country's biggest church.

From Beethoven to Liszt

Work on building the Basilica of Esztergom began in 1822. Ludwig van Beethoven offered to conduct his Missa Solemnis for the consecration — but he died before the church was completed. In fact, the consecration was delayed until 1856, awaiting completion of the dome, by which time a new, home-grown musical genius had emerged on the scene. Ferenc (Franz) Liszt thus baptized the new basilica with his specially composed Esztergom Mass (also known as the Gran Mass in Germany). Even Liszt's baptism was premature, however: the basilica was not finally finished until 1869.

tion of religious objects, including a crystal cross from the 9th century and the 15th-century *Calvary* of King Mátyás. A higher climb up the tower takes you from priceless treasures to priceless views. Esztergom unfolds beneath your feet, and on good days you can also see all the way to Slovakia.

Alongside the basilica, the remains of a medieval royal palace have been excavated and restored to form the **Castle Museum**. Among the building's highlights are St. Stephen's Hall, the frescoed Hall of Virtues (Prudence, Temperance, Fortitude, and Justice), and the 12th-century Royal Chapel.

The most popular collection in Esztergom lies at the foot of Basilica Hill, on the riverside. The **Christian Museum** (Keresztény Múzeum) is one of the best religious art museums in the country. Covering mostly the Gothic and Renaissance periods from the 13th to the 16th centuries, it has a number of very good 14th- and 15th-century Italian paintings. Also notable is the 15th-century Coffin of Garamszentbenedek, an intricately carved and painted devotional vehicle, once paraded in the streets at Easter.

Lake Balaton

Though Hungary has no coastline, Lake Balaton is the next best thing. This massive freshwater lake is surrounded by verdant hills, orchards, vineyards, and historic villages. The northwestern tip of Balaton lies about 100 km (62 miles) from Budapest, making it a comfortable day-trip from the capital. Buses and trains serve the lake resort area, and coach excursions visit extensively in summer months.

Balaton is the largest lake in central and western Europe, measuring 77 km (48 miles) across, with an area of nearly 600 sq km (230 sq miles). Yet its average depth is only 3 m (10 ft). In winter it freezes over completely, while in summer the shallow water is subject to wind-driven waves; when a storm blows up even the ferries call it a day.

However, for most of the summer, the sun warms the tranquil lake almost to air temperature, attracting swimmers by the thousands. The mildly alkaline water is said to be healthy for bathing. Balaton authorities ensure that the lake is kept clean and calm by banning motor boats (the few exceptions require special permits).

About 40 species of fish thrive in Balaton, a sure sign of the lake's cleanliness. Balaton pike-perch (*fogas*) is usually singled out as the tastiest and is a popular dish on menus both here and in the capital. Fishermen operate from shore, from boats, and from platforms set a little distance into the lake. Agriculture flourishes all along the

A smiling Budapesti is a common sight, not just in the countryside but in the city, too.

circumference of the lake; the area blossoms with fruit trees, rippling fields of wheat and, in the area of Badacsony, some of the finest vineyards in Hungary.

The north and south shores of the lake have very distinct personalities. The northern shore shelves quicker and, in many places, is less suited to bathing than the southern shore. The north, popular with families and older visitors, is backed by hills, greenery, and quaint villages; the south is flatter and better suits younger and more hedonistic visitors interested in discos and resort-style facilities.

The North Shore

Approaching Balaton from Budapest and navigating the lake in a counter-clockwise direction (along the perimeter Highway 71), you will come to Balatonalmádi, the first settlement of any size. The parish church has a medieval chapel, but most people come here to enjoy the beach — the biggest and one of the best-equipped along the northern shore, with space for 12,000 sunbathing bodies. Signs for the beach read "Strand", but that won't guarantee you a sandy or even pebbly stretch of beach — it simply means the lake edge, which may be of sand, lawn, or even concrete.

Balatonfüred, some 13 km (8 miles) farther west, has been a spa area since Roman times. The main square, called **Gyógy tér** (meaning "Health" or "Therapeutic Square"), is a handsome place where the local mineral water bubbles up from the ground beneath a pagoda-like well-head. Grand old buildings stand on three sides of the square: the 18th-century Horváth House, once an inn and now a miner's sanatorium; the Trade Union Sanatorium of 1802; and the Cardiac Hospital, which has treated heart patients from all over the world. The small grove in front of the square has a number

Those in search of Riviera-style leisure will find a more serene equivalent around Lake Balaton.

of trees dedicated by personalities who have visited here, including the late prime minister of India, Indira Gandhi.

Leading from the square is the street called **Blaha Lujza utca**, with a fine 1867 villa. On the opposite side of the road is the best café on the lake: Kedves has been going strong for two centuries, in no small part due to its fantastic chocolate cake. At the end of this street is a rotunda church built in the 1840s and a small museum to the Hungarian author Mór Jókai (closed November to February). Balatonfüred is one of the lake's liveliest resorts, bustling by day and night.

One of the most attractive spots on Lake Balaton is the village of **Tihany**, on a peninsula that nearly divides the lake in two and ends at the ferry point of Tihanyi-rév, where there is a Club Med-style camp and hotel. The unspoiled **peninsula** is protected by National Park status. It even has its own small lake, popular with bird-watchers and nature lovers. To the south are the domes of former geysers.

The village sits high on a hill above the main lake. The principal street, Pisky sétány (a promenade), has a few charming traditional thatched houses. Just below this point, and slightly removed from the main road, is the **Abbey Church** (Apátság). The present 18th-century baroque church stands over an atmospheric crypt approaching a thousand years in age. A rare survivor in a land constantly ravaged by so many invasions, it is thought to be the oldest in Hungary. The crypt houses the tomb of King András (Andrew) I who founded the Benedictine abbey that stood on this site in 1055.

Next door to the Abbey Church, housed in the old priory, is the **Tihany Historical Museum** (closed November to February). The museum features regional folk items and art; three small rooms where Hungary's last king, Károly IV, lived for five days in 1921; and, in the basement, an atmospheric lapidarium containing Roman remains. In front of the church, King András is commemorated in an offbeat statue by Imre Varga, wrapped in an aluminum cloak.

Some of the quaint white thatched houses that run along Pisky sétány have been converted into a **Museum of Ethnography** (similar to the one at Szentendre, but on a much smaller scale). In the Fishermen's House, for example, you can see canoes and fishing equipment used on the lake until the 1930s (museum closed November to April).

A promenade overlooking the lake passes restaurants and craft and souvenir shops before terminating at Echo

Tihany is a good starting point for exploring the eastern shores of Lake Balaton's peninsula on foot.

Hill, where the views are the main attraction. A marked path continues to the *óvár* — not a castle, as the name suggests, but a volcanic outcrop dotted with cells made by monks.

The **Badacsony** region is as inextricably linked with Hungary's wine industry as Burgundy is to that of France or Napa Valley to that of California. The wines, though, may take a back seat to the fine scenery that greets visitors here. The region's volcanic past is evident as soon as you catch sight of the conical green hills. Mount Badacsony, the central basalt peak and the largest of the extinct volcanoes (437 m/1,434 ft), is invariably described as "coffin-shaped." The basalt "organ-pipes" of **Szentgyörgyhegy** are an especially fine sight. Fit and energetic visitors may wish to hike up these hills, but the easy way is by car, or by a jeep that shuttles passengers to and from the bottom of the hill to the wine museum and three small museum houses, as well as scenic points of interest.

A little way farther west, set back from the main road, is the small settlement of **Szigliget**. The moody remains of a 13th-century castle offer fine views of the village and lake.

The last town on the north shore, **Keszthely** (pronounced "*kest-hey*"), was once owned entirely by the wealthy Festetics family during the 18th and 19th centuries. The family's **palace** is one of Hungary's most important baroque monuments (open all year round). The highlight is the Helikon library, claimed to be the grandest in the country, and it alone is worth the palace entrance charge.

Continuing out of Keszthely to the southwest on Highway 71, you reach another good historical collection. The **Balaton Museum** portrays the story of the settlement of the lake and the development of its people, including their agricultural and fishing practices, and the lake's flora and fauna.

The South Shore

Near the southwest corner of the lake, Kis-Balaton (Little Balaton), a marshy National Reserve, is noted for its rare birdlife. Observation towers are provided for bird watchers.

Fonyód is the second largest of the south shore resorts, and ferries run from here to Badacsony. A better place to stay might be **Balatonföldvár**, arguably the area's most attractive resort, well-landscaped around parks and gardens.

At Szántód, the lake is squeezed to its narrowest point by the Tihany peninsula. Cars invariably queue here to make the 10-minute crossing to the north shore. On the other side, almost due south of the ferry point, is **Szántódpuszta**, where traditional life on the country's Great Plain is evoked in 30 buildings dating from the 18th and 19th centuries, including farm buildings, a church, and a *csárda* (rustic restaurant). Craft displays are given at regular interrvals.

The largest town on the lake's south coast is **Siófok**, which boasts a *strand* (beach) attracting thousands of sunbathers and offering a lively nightlife. Pleasure craft depart from the large harbor, but the most pleasant stretch of waterfront is to be found in the gardens immediately east of the port. The town center, which has a small museum of local history is found further east, just before the hotel zone.

Red paprika drying in the summer sunshine is a common sight in rural Hungary.

Bathtime in Budapest

Budapest is built on a bed of more than 100 natural hot water springs, and its steam-bath (*fürdő*) tradition can be traced all the way back to the Romans. The Ottoman Empire left little by way of a permanent legacy from its 150 years of occupation, other than a handful of Turkish baths, several of which are still operating today, virtually unchanged since the Middle Ages. There are about 30 *fürdő* in Budapest and, although they specialize in curing all manner of ailments, most Budapestis go simply for a social soak and to unwind.

The Gellért and the Széchenyi baths are the grandest of them all, art nouveau and neo-classical palaces respectively, with splendid baths and outdoor pools. For non-Hungarian speakers, these mixed-sex complexes are also the most accessible. Once you've got the hang of what's on offer, try the other baths (the 15th and 16th-century Király, Rác, or Rudas) for true local atmosphere. The experience can be remarkably transporting in these ancient baths, where sunlight filters through holes in the domed ceilings, and stone arches ring the octagonal pools. By contrast, the Palatinus Strand on Maragaret is more like a giant water park, ideal for families.

A basic three-hour session costs from 800 to 1600 forints, with other treatments costing extra. These will be listed on a noticeboard in the foyer next to the ticket booth, but in most cases in Hungarian only. Don't expect attendants to speak more than a couple of words of English or German, if that. The most basic services are *termál* (for access to the thermal baths and pool), *fürdő* (bath) and *masszírozás* (massage). If you're having difficulty, a request for *termál* ("*tear-mal*") should get you admitted to both thermal baths and the swimming pool.

Inside the locker room you will be given a towel and a thin cotton thong or apron to cover up, as well as a metal disc that corresponds to any additional treatment you have paid for. An attendant will show you to a locker (frequently a walk-in cabin, for which you pay extra at the Gellért); remember your number, so that the attendant can reopen the locker when you leave.

Feel free to move among the thermal pools, steam baths and brisk cold pools at will, following the example of locals. At single-sex baths, nude bathing is *de riguer*. At the mixed-sex baths (where the thermal baths are segregated), you will need a bathing suit for the pools.

It's a good idea to take a (waterproof) money pouch in with you, as tipping can work wonders, making the experience even more worthwhile. In the swimming pools, you are expected to wear a bathing cap, which you can either obtain free or for a minimal fee.

Men especially should be aware that a couple of the single-sex baths are extremely popular with Budapest's gay crowd. Rác (in particular on Saturday afternoons) and, to a lesser extent, Király, are prime cruising ground.

For additional information, pick up the brochure and map *Budapest Baths/Bäder* at any Tourinform office.

Rudas: Döbrentei tér 9; Tel. 456-1322; thermal baths open to men only, Mon–Fri, 6am–7pm; Sat–Sun, 6am–noon; pool open to men and women (same hours). Tram: 18, 19.

Rác: Hadnagy u. 8–10; Tel. 356-1322; open to women Mon, Wed & Fri, 6:30am–7pm; to men, Tue, Thur, Sat 6:30am–7pm. Tram: 18.

Gellért: Kelenhegyi út 2-4; Tel. 466-6166; open to men and women; baths daily 6am–6pm; pool Sat–Sun, 6am–4pm. Tram: 18, 19, 47, or 49.

Király: Fő u. 84; Tel. 202-3688; open to women, Tue & Thur, 6:30am–6pm, Sat 6:30–noon; to men, Mon, Wed & Fri, 9am–8pm. Metro: Batthány tér.

Lukács: Frankel Leó u. 25-29; Tel. 326-1695; open to men and women, Mon–Fri, 6am–7pm Sat–Sun, 6am–5pm. Tram: 4, 6, 17.

Széchenyi: Állatkerti körút 11; Tel. 321-0310; open to men and women, Mon–Fri, 6am–7pm; Sat–Sun, 6am–5pm. Metro: Széchenyi fürdő.

Palatinus Strand: Margitsziget; Tel. 112-3069; open to men and women, daily 8am–7pm. Bus: 26.

WHAT TO DO

SHOPPING

Only a few years ago, dollar-wielding tourists were treated like privileged royalty on the shopping streets of Budapest. Now, with the post-Communist imposition of a general sales tax (ÁFA, or VAT) of 25 percent, and high inflation, Budapest is no longer the bargain-basement spot it once was, though it is still cheaper than most Western European capitals.

Where to Shop

Hungary's emergence from Communism and the development of a market economy have produced a proliferation of

Tax Refunds

Foreigners are eligible to reclaim the Hungarian national sales tax (ÁFA) of up to 25 percent on single-store purchases above 50,000 Ft. (except on purchases of art and antiques). Look for the blue-and-white "Tax Free for Tourists" signs, posted in participating shops. When you depart from Hungary, cash refunds can be claimed at IBUSZ offices at the airport and Keleti Railway Station, and refunds can also be made to credit cards. Visitors must present the purchase along with the AFA refund claim and original invoice (in the Tax Free envelope) to the customs officer upon departure. These forms are obtained from the participating store where the purchase is made. For additional information on obtaining refunds, contact Global Refund Hungary (Bég u 3-5; Tel/fax 212-4906 or 800/KNOW-VAT; <www.globalrefund.com>).

stores and boutiques, including many selling consumer goods imported from Western Europe and North America. You can now buy most Western goods in the city's department stores, specialist shops, and market stalls.

Handpainted Easter eggs make a colorful souvenir of Hungarian folk art.

Many visitors begin their shopping expeditions on **Váci utca**, the most comprehensive and chic shopping street in Budapest (see page 46). The pedestrian-only boulevard has a wide selection of shops selling clothes, fashion accessories, shoes, jewelry, antiques, books, music, china, glass, and much more. Be sure to continue on to the lower section of Váci utca (beyond Erzébet Bridge), where the street has recently been converted to pedestrian-only. Budapest's newest and largest mall, with 400 shops and a luxury hotel, is the **Westend City Center** (Váci út 1–3; Tel. 238-7777), next to the Nyugati Train Station.

For folk art and other handcrafts, start at **Folkart Centrum** (Váci utca 14; Tel. 318-5840). This branch, the biggest and best of a small chain of outlets, is open daily. You will also find folk goods sold at Tárnok utca 8 and stalls around Vörösmarty tér and Vigadó tér (though the stalls at the former, especially, are reputed to be overpriced). Ask Tourinform for directions to the massive **Ecseri Flea Market** (Nagykőösi út 156), which has a wide variety of items, including famous porcelain and ceramics and religious icons (Tuesday to Saturday).

The free monthly magazine, *Where Budapest*, features individual store listings.

What to Buy

Ceramics and Porcelain: Hungary is celebrated for its ceramics and porcelain, and the two leading manufacturers are Herend, made in the town of the same name near Lake Balaton, and Zsolnay, made in the south of Hungary. The Herend factory has been producing fine porcelain for the tables of the nobility since 1826; members of the British royal family from Queen Victoria to Charles and Diana have been customers. Everything is still hand-finished, so prices are not cheap. You don't need to travel all the way to Herend to buy Herend porcelain and pottery, though; there is a specialist shop on József Nádor tér 11 (behind the Gerbeaud café on Vörösmarty tér). You can buy Zsolnay porcelain at the shop of the same name on V. Kígyó utca 4.

More affordable folk-style plates and vases are common, including distinctive blue-and-white ware, ochre and floral-decorated glazed water jars from Mezötúr, and local charcoal-colored items, called "black pottery." Informal kitchen pottery can be had at Herend Village Pottery (Bem rakpart 37).

Chess sets: You will find beautiful gift sets for sale in souvenir shops along Váci utca. Pawns in the guise of foot soldiers and knights as hussars in bright 18th-century garb are but one variation.

Food and drink: Paprika in small gift boxes or sachets, strudels packed in sturdy cardboard boxes, salami, goose liver paté, Hungarian wines (particularly Tokaj) and liqueurs (such as apricot brandy) are popular gifts, and cost much less than elsewhere in Europe. For wine, try House of Hungarian Wines (Szentháromság tér 6), which stocks some 400 different varieties from across the country and conducts tastings, and Budapest Wine Society (Battyány utca 59; Tel. 212-2569), in Buda.

Wine-bottle stoppers in Hungarian style.

Russian dolls: Hardly Hungarian, but a solid symbol of old Eastern and Central Europe, Russian figures are everywhere. If you buy the popular doll of Russian leaders, you get a miniature history lesson to boot: hidden inside Yeltsin is Gorbachev, inside Gorbachev is Andropov, and so on.

Soviet army memorabilia: Many markets and craft stalls sell relics of the Soviet era: fur hats, steel helmets, cap badges, and watches. You can buy T-shirts celebrating Communism's demise at Statue Park.

Textiles and Embroidery: Embroidered and handspun blouses, tablecloths, lace, blankets, and carpets can be purchased at Folkart shops or at stalls set up in small towns in the countryside. Of particular interest are intricate Halas lace, Matyó needlework and costumes, red-and-blue Palóc embroidery (aprons, towels and kerchiefs), and Kalocsa embroidered folk costumes. Because these hand-embroidered items involve a high degree of handiwork, prices can be high.

Woodwork: Boxes, bowls, walking sticks, and other hand-carved items are fairly

> Addresses in Budapest are a little tricky. For example, "V., Markó u 72 II/44" means "District V (ie 5), Markó utca (ie Markó street), house number 72, second floor, apartment number 44."

common. Look for the fascinating "secret boxes," frequently sold by the Roma, or Gypsies. You'll also find a variety of children's toys, including puzzles and mobiles, made from wood, just like in the good old days.

ENTERTAINMENT

Budapest has always had a very active nightlife. Now more cosmopolitan than ever, the city overflows with options. Budapest is perhaps best known for highbrow culture: theater, opera, ballet, and particularly classical concerts. Tickets for such performances are much more democratically priced than in many parts of the world. Those with a particular interest in music, be it classical or folk, should try to time their visits to coincide with one of the city's major cultural festivals, such as the Spring Festival, which draws hundreds of performers from around the world for three weeks' worth of top-drawer concerts and shows (see "Calendar of Events" on page 93).

The grandeur of the State Opera House is echoed in the performances that take place here.

Budapest also has a wide array of popular cultural offerings, ranging from Parisian-style cabarets to smoky jazz sessions and raunchy exotic dancer shows. Big-name international pop and rock bands don't make as many appearances as they used to, since the largest indoor concert venue burned down and is not likely to be rebuilt or replaced for several years. However, one of Europe's largest rock festivals takes place in Budapest every summer.

Performing Arts: Budapestis are stalwart supporters of the fine arts. On average, several new productions give premières in Hungary each week. The **Hungarian State Opera House** on Andrássy út 20 (Tel. 331-2550) is the finest of the city's dedicated opera venues and connoisseurs rank it among Europe's best. Tickets are available at the box office (Tel. 332-7914; <www.opera.hu>).

The city has a number of other fine halls (*színház*) for symphonies, concerts and opera, including the **Ferenc Liszt Academy of Music** (Liszt Ferenc tér 8; Tel. 342-0179), a splendid art nouveau music hall built in 1904, and **Pesti Vigadó** (Vigadó tér 1; Tel. 266-6177).

Except for performances at the English-language **Merlin Theater** (Gerlóczy utca 4, Tel. 317-9338), dramatic plays are staged in Hungarian, thus excluding almost all foreign tourists.

Ballet is performed at the **Erkel Theatre** (Köztársaság tér 30; Tel. 333-0540) and at the **Nemzeti Színház** (National Theatre) on Hevesi Sándor tér. In August the **Budafest** is a spectacular celebration of opera and ballet in the State Opera House. Other classical music venues include **St. Stephen's Basilica** and the **Béla Bartók Memorial House** (Csalán út 29; Tel. 394-2100).

Popular mainstream musicals from Broadway and London's West End (like *Cats, Les Misérables,* etc.) can be enjoyed in Budapest, as long as you don't mind a little Hungarian in between the songs. The **Thália Theatre** (Nagymező utca 22-24; Tel. 312 4230) is one of the best venues to see dance musicals and other theater performances.

For pop, rock, and jazz concerts see the weekly *Style* supplement of the *Budapest Sun* or the monthly publication *Where Budapest*. Both contain good round-ups of bars, pubs, and clubs in the city.

Tickets are available at the following central locations: for opera and concert performances go to **Központi Jegyiroda**, or Central Ticket Office (Andrássy út 15; Tel. 267-9737, Monday–Friday 10am–6pm); for concert and theater tickets, **Publika** (Károly krt. 9, Tel. 322-2010; Monday-Friday 10am-6pm and Saturday, 10-2pm); and the **Vigadó Ticket Office**, on the ground floor of Vörösmarty tér 1 (tel. 317-6222). Tickets for rock concerts and jazz club shows are available from **Music Mix** (Váci utca 33, Tel. 317-7736; Monday–Friday, 10am–6pm, Saturday 10am–1pm).

Larger hotels will also make bookings for you, or you can simply go direct to the venue box office. A good free publication (in English) with listings is *Pesti Est*, available at box offices, hotels, and restaurants.

Clubs and Bars: Hungary's late-night drinking and partying scene is on a par with other international cities. Pubs, based either on the English model or the German bierstube, are found alongside international bars, Continental-style cafés, and authentic Hungarian bars, though few of the latter are apparent in the main tourist areas. Look for the sign *sörözo* if you are a beer drinker, and *borozó* if you prefer wine. While a sörözo is often similar to a German *bierstube*, a borozó is rarely like a Parisian wine bar (and neither serves only beer or wine). An excellent pub with a good beer selection is Portside (Dohány utca 7). Expats hang out at Becketts

(V. Bajcsy-Zsilinsky út 72), an Irish pub with good pub grub. Beer lovers will want to check out Belgian Brasserie (see page 136), with a superb range of Belgian beers and good, inexpensive food.

Live music is scheduled most nights of the week, with jazz (suppressed as subversive in the Stalinist era) currently enjoying something of a renaissance in Budapest nightspots. Most performances are blues and Dixieland, and audiences are generally young. One of the top venues, definitely on the bohemian side, is **Old Man's Music Pub** (Akácfa utca 13), which hosts a wide range of rock, blues and jazz performances for occasionally rowdy fans. There are also several

---

Táncház: the Folk Dance House Scene

Hungarian folk dance reaches its popular apex at nightclubs in the capital that promote táncház, an urban revival of traditional rural Magyar dance. Called a "dance house movement," it arose as an expression of protest and national pride during Communist rule in the 1970s and has produced some of the biggest names in Hungarian folk music. Transylvanian, southern Slav, Bulgarian, and Greek music and dance styles are also represented.

Most clubs offer lessons to visitors, although you may have just as much fun having a drink and watching the energetic folk dancing. No one worries about folk costume, and the crowd is young and trendy. Two clubs to check out are: Kalamajka Dance House, in downtown Pest (Molnar utca 9, near Ferenciek tere Metro; Tel. 317-5928) and Csángó Dance House at the Marcizbányi tér Mûvelõdési Ház in Buda (Marcizbányi tér 5/a, near the Moszkva tér metro; Tel. 212-0803). The National Dance House Festival takes place every March in Budapest.

---

cabaret clubs presenting floorshows with big-production numbers and scantily clad dancers.

Among Budapest's many cafés, two that blur the line between coffeehouse and bar are **Café Vian** (Liszt Ferenc tér 9) and **Pesti Est Café** (Liszt Ferenc tér 5). (For more sedate, traditional cafés, see the box on page 100.)

For visitors who prefer the excitement of the **casino**, Hungary has two dozen gambling establishments. The place to be seen is the **Hilton Hotel**, which (in common with most Budapest casinos) offers French and American roulette, blackjack, poker, punto banco, baccarat and slot machines. There are many other city casinos: among them are the **Las Vegas** in the Atrium Hyatt; the **Orfeum** in the Hotel Béke Radisson; the **Vigadó** on Vigadó utca; and the **Várkert** on the Buda embankment at the southern tip of Castle Hill. The latter is housed in a beautiful neo-Renaissance building by Miklós Ybl, designer of the Opera House. Casinos generally open from 4pm to 3 or 4am.

Film: Hungarians take their movies seriously, and Hungarian actors, auteurs and cinematographers have made impressive contributions to domestic, European and Hollywood films. Unfortunately, foreign visitors are better off waiting to catch Hungarian films in their home country, where they'll be subtitled. Many foreign films are subtitled in Hungary. Movie houses screening such films include the Corvin, Puskin Mozi, WestEnd Century, and Szindbád.

Folklore: Despite rapid modernization and the influx of cultural products from the West, Hungary continues to have a very active folk music and dance scene. Hungarian folk-dancing is lively and fascinating, and many performances escort visitors through the whole gamut, from courtly wedding dances to high-energy, boot-slapping "Lad's Dances" from the 18th century. These tend to be best at local festivals, where performers are there for the love of dancing or local pride. In the same vein, look out for authentic Gypsy dancers. One folkore group that has received a great deal of international attention — featured in the soundtrack for the film *The English Patient* — is Muzsikás. The group makes occasional appearances in Budapest, especially during Spring Festival.

You can see Hungarian dancers — amateur or professional — most nights at the Municipal Folklore Center at Fehérvári út 47, south of Gellért Hill. Folklore evenings are also staged at a number of venues; the Hungarian State Folk Ensemble gives excellent performances. Folklore evenings of a different type are also touted by some restaurants, though these tend to be staged for tour groups and are not always representative of authentic Hungarian folk entertainment.

SPORTS

For a small nation, Hungary has enjoyed significant Olympic and World Championship success. During the 1950s its football (soccer) team was one of the finest in the world. Once Communism promoted national sport as proof of the might of the State, and restricted many sports facilities to the athletic elite, but Hungary now offers many sports options to spectators and active participants alike.

Cycling: Budapest has nearly 100 km (62 miles) of bicycle paths throughout the city (including along Andrássy út), and City Park, Margaret Island and the Buda Hills are made for enthusiastic cyclists. Pick up a copy of the Budapest for Bikers' Map if you're looking to do some serious cycling. You can rent bikes in City Park and on Margaret Island.

Horseback riding: Hungarians have been known for their equestrian prowess ever since the Magyars swept over the Great Plain. Several good stables and horse-riding schools are available to visitors. Most are located just outside Budapest. Riding can be arranged through the Budapesti Equestrian Club (Kerepesi út 7; Tel. 313-5210), Aranypatkó Lovarda Riding School (Aranyhegi út 18; Tel. 387-7152) and Petneházy Riding Center (Fekefefej utca 2–4; Tel. 397-5048). Ask Tourinform for details, visit Pegazus Tours on Fereciek tere, or see the IBUSZ brochure, Riding in Hungary. You could also contact the Hungarian Equestrian Tourism Association at Fereciek tere 4 (Tel. 317-1644; <www.gak.hu/equi>).

Ice skating: The large lake in the City Park is turned into an ice rink in winter (November–March, Monday–Friday, 9am–1pm and 4pm–8pm; Saturday and Sunday, 10am–2pm and 4pm–8pm), against the romantic backdrop of the Vajdahunyad Castle.

Swimming: Swimmers have an excellent selection of pools at the varied thermal bath complexes across the city. (See the feature on page 78 for additional information.)

Tennis: There are a very view public courts, though some three dozen hotels in Budapest have courts. Several clubs have both indoor and outdoor courts. Visitors can arrange court time through Budapest Sports Club (Szamos u 2; Tel. 317-4762; 12 courts); MTK Tennis Club (Bartók Béla út 63; Tel. 209-1595, 19 courts), and Vasas Sport Club (Pasaréti út 11–13; Tel. 355-7650, 21 courts).

Watersports: Windsurfing and yachting are widely practiced on Lake Balaton; boats and boards can be hired at the main resorts.

Spectator Sports

Grand Prix: The major event of the year is the annual Formula I Grand Prix meeting at the Hungaroring, about 19 km (12 miles) east of Budapest.

Football (soccer): Football is Hungary's most popular spectator sport. Two of the most popular of Budapest's first-division football teams are Kispest-Honvéd (which plays at Bozsik stadium; Tel. 282-9789) and Ferencváros (FTC stadium; Tel. 215-1013). The latter has a somewhat thuggish minority among its supporters.

Horseracing: The Lóverseny tér stadium (at Kerepesi út 11) is the main venue for horseracing and attracts a large audience. Flat race meetings take place on Sundays and Thursdays in summer.

CHILDREN'S BUDAPEST

The best place for children in Budapest is City Park, where the zoo and amusement park lie within a few yards of each other, and the circus makes regular appearances. The splendid Széchenyi Baths, with its Olympic and outdoor

Luxuriating in one of Budapest's 30 ancient spa baths is a sociable way to soak and unwind.

thermal pools, are sure to satisfy both restless kids and their rest-deprived parents. In summer there's a boating lake in the park, which becomes an ice-skating rink in winter.

The other oasis in the city is Margaret Island. You can spend a good hour or so riding round it *en famille* on a bicycle-carriage made for four. You can also swim here in the city's biggest baths, the Palatinus Strand. Children are certain to enjoy the open-air wave pool there and at the Gellért Hotel in Buda. Out of town, Lake Balaton is a good place for water babies, particularly the southern edge where the sandy shore slopes gently into warm water.

An 1874 cog-wheel railway and a small-gauge children's train travel to the peaceful Buda hills (see page 43). The chairlift to János Hill is also a perennial favorite among youngsters. Children may also enjoy taking the funicular up to Castle Hill, and walking across the Chain Bridge — especially at night when the bridge, the Parliament building and the Royal Palace are all illuminated.

Older children with an interest in horses may enjoy a day at a riding school (see page 87) or one of the tour operators' organized horse shows. Details are available from IBUSZ or Tourinform.

Sitting on daddy's shoulders on a visit to City Park makes me feel almost as tall as one of the Zoo's giraffes.

Calendar of Events

Dates of events and festivals appear in *Where Budapest* and other bulletins, and can be obtained from Tourinform and IBUSZ offices.

February. *Filmszemle*: A 10-day event during which new Hungarian films are screened at the Budapest Convention Center. *Opera Ball*: at the Hungarian State Opera House.

March. *Budapest Spring Festival*: two weeks of the best in Hungarian music, theater, dance, and art. *Spring Days*: historical dramas enacted at Szentendre.

May. *Book Week*: a carnival atmosphere prevails as bookstalls sprout up all over Budapest selling the new season's books. End of May.

June–July. *Summer concert season*: Budapest's open-air cinemas begin their screenings, and theaters stage light drama, musicals, opera, operetta, and revues. *Danube Flower Carnival*: second week in June. *Ferencváros Summer Festival*. *Jewish Summer Festival*.

August. *Saint Stephen's Day*: (20th) processions, *Craftsmen's Fair* in the Castle District, and firework display on Gellért Hill. *Budafest*: celebration of opera and ballet in the State Opera House. *Wine Harvest Celebration*: popular wine festival in Boglárlelle near Lake Balaton. *Hungarian Grand Prix*: Formula 1 cars race at the Hungaroring circuit. *Pepsi Island*: huge outdoor, week-long popular music festival on Óbuda Island. *National Jewish Festival*: music and art with Jewish themes.

September. *Budapest International Wine Festival*: wine-tasting stalls at Vörösmarty tér, festivities and parade. *Wine harvest*: Badacsony on Lake Balaton.

September/October. *Autumn Festival, Budapest Arts Weeks*: music, theatre, dance, and fine arts events take place at venues around the city, with renowned participants from all over the world.

EATING OUT

Hungarians take pride in their food and drink, and their cuisine has a rich history, but few people outside Hungary know much about Magyar cuisine, besides paprika and goulash. Goulash, the most famous Hungarian dish, is actually most often served as a thick soup. Paprika, the mild pepper spice, is a staple of most Hungarian households and restaurants. Hungarian cooking is predominantly peasant food: rich, heavy and high in calories, served in large portions.

Budapest has exploded with a profusion of new restaurants, and the dining scene is more varied, cosmopolitan and exciting than ever.

WHERE TO EAT

You won't often see the sign "restaurant" in Budapest; if you do, the establishment is likely to cater to foreign tourists. The two most common names for an eatery are *étterem* and *vendéglõ*. A *csárda* (pronounced "*chard-a*") is normally a country inn complete with regional atmosphere. Others are *sörözo*, roughly translated as beer-hall, and *borozó*, or wine-bar. Both are usually just informal restaurants, and those attached to expensive hotels can be particularly good value. Budapest has long rivaled Vienna for its café culture and natives' love of pastries and coffee. Many cafés (*kávéház* and *cukrászda*) serve full meals as well as delectable cakes.

WHEN TO EAT

Breakfast (*reggeli*) is generally served between 7 and 10am. Hungarians generally don't eat much at the start of the day, but at most upscale hotels, a basic international breakfast buffet is generally served. Often you will find local pastries and possibly some foods you may not think of as usual breakfast fare, such as stuffed cabbage and other more hearty regional specialties.

Lunch (*ebéd*), generally served between 1 and 2 or 3pm, is the main meal of the day for Hungarians, a fact reflected in the quantities that tend to be served at midday.

Dinner (*vacsora*) is served between 7 and 10pm or later, though Hungarians in general are not late eaters. The menu is no less extensive than at lunchtime.

An array of local liquors and serving bottles in a range of bright colours, all intended to tempt visitors.

Hungarian cuisine

The first Magyars cooked their food in a pot over an open fire on the Great Plain, and many of today's dishes still retain that earthy rusticity. In the 17th century paprika arrived to spice up the diet — some say in the hands of fleeing Southern Slavs, others say the Turks brought it, while others contend that it came over from America. However it got to Hungary, paprika is a relatively mild seasoning; it should not be confused with the hotter-tasting chili. Paprika is an important element in Magyar cooking, but it is by no means used in every dish.

> Most restaurants provide an English translation of the menu, though you may find occasional eateries popular with locals that have no translation or one only in German.

Most food is cooked in lard rather than oil or butter (some restaurants cook only in goose fat). This tends to give it a heavier, richer taste than many Westerners are accustomed to. If Magyar portions are too hefty for you, order soup and then an appetizer instead of the main course.

Snacks: Hungarians love *lángos*, which is nothing more than deep-fried batter — made more enticing by spreading garlic, cheese and sour cream on it. There are stands serving up lángos at markets across Budapest.

Starters *(eloételek)*: Goose-liver paté and *hideg libamáj*, cold slices of goose liver served in its own fat on toast with purple onion rings, are perennial Hungarian favorites (the latter is also served as a main course). Pancakes *(crêpes)* Hortobágy-style are filled with minced meat, deep-fried until crispy, and dressed with sour cream. Budapest is also a good place to try caviar *(kaviár)*. The best is often Caspian.

Soups *(leves)*: Soups are immensely popular with locals and always on the menu. The well-known *gulyásleves* (goulash soup) is the standard bearer: chunks of beef, potatoes, onions, tomatoes, and peppers are cooked with paprika, garlic, and caraway for added flavor. Fishermen's soup *(halászlé)* is also based on potatoes, onions, tomatoes, and paprika, with the addition of chunks of freshwater fish. Also popular — and actually a meal in itself — is *babgulyás*, goulash soup served with dried beans. If you prefer lighter soup, try consommé with quail eggs *(eroleves fürjtojással)*. You're also likely to run across garlic cream soup served in its own hollowed-out bread loaf.

Perhaps the most intriguing "soup" of all is *hideg meggyleves* (cold sour-cherry soup). Topped with a frothy head of whipped cream, it would certainly be classified as a dessert elsewhere. On a hot day, try *hideg almaleves* — a creamy and refreshing cold apple soup, served with a dash of cinnamon.

Meat (*húsételek*): Hungary is a nation of avid carnivores. *Pörkölt* is the Hungarian stew that most closely approximates the West's notion of "goulash." It can be made with beef, chicken or pork. *Maharpörkölt* is beef stew and *borjúpörkölt* is veal stew; the list is as long as the meats available. Veal and pork are the top choice of most Hungarians, whether fried, stewed, or stuffed with different combinations of ham, cheese, mushrooms, or asparagus. Steaks, too, are always on the menu. *Lecsó* is steak accompanied by a stew of peppers, tomatoes,

Goulash may be a visitor's obvious choice, but there's much more on the menu

and onions. *Töltött káposzta* is another classic dish: cabbage leaves stuffed with pork and rice, served over sauerkraut with spicy sausage, paprika and a fattening dollop of sour cream.

Game and fowl: Game is very popular, as you might expect from the national affinity for meat and rich tastes. Wild boar (*vaddisznó*) and venison (*öz*) frequently appear on the menu, often reasonably priced. Chicken (*csirke*) is popular and inexpensive, and *csirke-paprikás* — chicken stewed with onion, green pepper, tomato, sour cream, and paprika — ranks as something of a national dish. Goose is another Magyar favorite, prized for more than its liver. Turkey often comes stewed or in stuffed portions, Kiev-style (garlic butter) or cordon bleu-style (ham and cheese). Look out too for stag, hare, pheasant, and wild duck.

Fish (*halételek*): Local fish in this land-locked country is necessarily of the freshwater variety; *ponty* (carp) and *fogas* (pike-perch from Lake Balaton) are the two most commonly found in Budapest. Even their ardent fans would admit that the taste of these is "delicate" and lovers of seafish may find them somewhat bland. A tasty fish soup, served with paprika, is *halászlé*.

Fresh fish, simply grilled or baked, is often priced per 10g or dekagram (dkg). An average portion is a quarter-kilo, so simply multiply by 25.

Vegetables and pasta: Vegetarian restaurants and vegetarian dishes are still a rarity on Hungarian menus. Vegetable accompaniments usually have to be ordered separately and can be uninspired. *Saláta* may be little more than an unexciting plate of cabbage and pickled beets. What most Westerners call a mixed salad usually appears as *vitamin saláta*. Strict vegetarians will need to monitor the menu closely: classic dishes of stuffed pepper (*töltött paprika*) and stuffed cabbage (*töltött káposzta*) include pork in the filling, and many soups that would appear to be meatless are not.

Some dishes are served with boiled potatoes, while most are eaten with pasta, either in ribbon noodles (*nokedli*) or more commonly in the form of a heavy starchy dumpling (*galuska*), often translated as "gnocchi" on the English menu.

Desserts (*tészták*): Hungarians are great eaters of pastries and sweets. Two desserts are ubiquitous in Budapest. One is the Gundel pancake (*Gundel palacsinta*), named after Hungary's most famous restaurateur. It is filled with nut and raisin paste, drenched in chocolate and rum sauce, and (if stated on the menu) flambéed. The equally calorific *somlói galuska* is a heavy sponge affair with vanilla, nuts, chocolate and whipped cream in an orange and rum sauce.

Strudels (*rétes*) clearly reveal an Austrian influence. Some items on the dessert menu are less identifiable as sweets. For example, *sztrapacska* combines pasta with curd cheese, sour cream and fried cubes of pork fat. For simpler tastes, there is always ice cream (*fagylalt*), cheese (*sajt*), or fruit (*gyümölcs*).

At Budapest's cafés, you can sample such goodies as pound cake, Sachertorte, truffle cake, carrot cake … the list goes on and on.

Drinks

Hungarian wines: The Great Plain, in southern Hungry, produces a great range of wines, from vigorous and full-bodied reds to smoky dry whites. The most famous of the white wines is Tokay (Tokaj), a rich aged dessert wine. The grapes used to produce this world-renowned wine are grown in the volcanic soil of the Tokay region in the northeast of

The coffee-house culture is easy to adopt, not just for its atmosphere, but for the taste as well.

The Budapest Kávéház

There's no more stylish way to put on the calories than at one of Budapest's coffeehouses (*kávéház*), where locals love to congregate, drink coffee and down incomparable sweets. Prices are inexpensive by Western standards.

The grand dame of the city is without doubt **Gerbeaud** (Vörösmarty tér 7), the luxuriously ornate haunt of the city's elite since 1870. It has excellent cakes and pastries, great people-watching on the terrace and notoriously diffident service. **New York Kávéház** (Erzsébet krt. 9–11), is a *belle époque* beauty, despite being trapped in exterior scaffolding for several decades. It once played host to the city's literary and artistic elite.

The charmingly old-world **Café Muvész** (Andrássy út 29, near the Opera House) serves excellent pastries amid chandeliers, giant gilded mirrors and marble tabletops. Down the street, the regal **Lukács** (Andrássy út 70) has reopened after a loving restoration. Another legendary café that was brought back to life in 2000, after lying dormant for a half century, is **Centrál Kávéház** (Károlyi Mihály út 9, near Ferenc ter). The café first opened in 1887 and it serves excellent coffee, pastries and affordable meals. It even has a large non-smoking section.

On Castle Hill, cozy **Ruszwurm** (Szentháromság utca 7, one block from Matthias Church) continues its tradition of excellent cakes and relaxed pace even as hordes of tourists peer in its windows. **Angelika Kávéház** (Batthyány tér 7) is another handsome traditional café replete with wood paneling and mirrors, offering a large selection of Hungarian and Viennese pastries.

Most coffeehouses stay open until 10 or 11pm, though New York, Muvész and Centrál are open until midnight.

Hungary. The grapes are left on the vine until autumn mists encourage the growth of the noble rot that gives the wine its intense sweetness and complex character. Tokay has been produced for over 200 years, and the wine was a favorite of Catherine the Great and Louis XIV; it also inspired poetry from Voltaire and music from Schubert. Tokaji Furmint is dry, Tokaji Szamorodni is medium sweet, akin to sherry, and Tokaji Aszú is full-bodied and sweet.

Less celebrated but perfectly satisfying white table wines come from the Lake Balaton region, including Rieslings, Sauvignon Blancs and Chardonnays. Badacsonyi wines are the best known and have been enjoyed for some 2,000 years. Some of the best white wines in the country come from its smallest wine-producing region, Somló.

The Villány region produces some of Hungary's biggest reds, many of which are aged in oak casks, including the fine Villányi burgundi and the very tannic Kékoportó. The most famous Hungarian red, which comes from the northeastern region, is the splendidly named "Egri Bikavér ("Bull's Blood of Eger") — a full-bodied and spicy accompaniment to many meat or game dishes. More subtle is the Pinot Noir from the same town.

Other drinks: There are no recognized Hungarian apéritifs, but a Puszta cocktail is as good a way as any to start the evening. It's a mixture of apricot brandy, local cognac-style brandy, and sweet Tokay wine.

Hungarian beers (*sör*) go well with heavy, spicy foods; except at the most formal of restaurants, it is as acceptable to drink beer with a meal as it is wine.

Finish off your evening with one of Hungary's famous fruit brandies (*pálinka*). They are fermented from the fruit and therefore have a clean, dry taste. The favorite is *barack* (apricot), followed by *cseresznye* (cherry). Claiming to be

the country's national drink, the peculiar green herbal liqueur called "Zwack Unicum", has been drunk for a couple of hundred years.

Coffee (*kávé*) is a favorite drink of Budapestis, but it is most commonly served black, hot, and sweet, espresso-style in thimble-sized cups. There used to be no alternative but now you'll find milk available everywhere, and cappuccino is served all over Budapest and in the large towns.

Not everyone in Budapest is coffee-mad. Tea is also commonly available, and a request for a pot of Earl Grey, or any other familiar types of tea — with lemon or milk — will raise no eyebrows in the city's better coffeehouses.

Linger over coffee and cakes at the Central Café.

Help with the Menu

gyümölc	fruit
halak	fish
húsételek	meat dishes
kenyér	bread
levesek	soup
sajt	cheese
saláták	salad
zöldság	vegetables

Preparations

csípos	hot (spicy)
fózött	boiled
hideg	cold
pörkölt	stew
sútve	baked/fried
agyonsütve	well-done
félig nyersen	rare
közepesen kisütve	medium

Meat & Poultry

bárány	lamb
borjú	veal
csirke	chicken
gulyás	goulash
kacsa	duck
liba	goose
marha	beef
sertés	pork

Fish

fogas	pike-perch
halászlé	fish stew
pisztráng	trout
ponty	carp
tonhal	tuna

Beverages

sör	beer
kávé	coffee
víz	water
fehér bor	white wine
vörös bor	red wine

HANDY TRAVEL TIPS
An A–Z Summary of Practical Information

A

ACCOMMODATION (See also YOUTH HOSTELS and RECOMMENDED HOTELS)

Hotels in Budapest are graded from one star to five stars, and those rating three to five are of comparable international standard. Until the last decade there was a shortage of good hotels in the city; while a number of excellent, if expensive, four-star establishments were built to fill that gap, there is still a dearth of good three-star hotels and few, if any, two- or one-star hotels that can be recommended. Budapest has a large number of top-flight, five-star hotels targeting business travelers and upscale tourists. While those are expensive, in general prices in Budapest lag behind those of other European capitals.

If all the higher grade hotels are full, or beyond your budget, the best option is to stay slightly out of town in a panzió (pension bed-and-breakfast hotel). Most are set in the Buda Hills — serenity, greenery, occasional great city views and lower cost are the trade-offs for being outside the city. Other options to consider are accommodation in private homes or a self-catering apartment. Neither of these are well developed for Western tourists within the city, but if you are feeling adventurous, contact the IBUSZ tourist information office for a list of addresses. Accommodation in private homes is, however, well-established in the Lake Balaton area, as the numerous German *zimmer* (room) signs indicate.

It is essential to book ahead during peak season (April to October). Tourinform tourist offices (including the one at the airport) will provide accommodation lists, but only IBUSZ offices (Vörösmarty tér 6, Tel. 317-3925; and at Keleti and Nyugati railway stations) provide a booking service.

If you want to be comfortable in July or August, make sure the room is equipped with air-conditioning (standard in four- and all five-star hotels). Note that many hotels quote prices in euros to compensate for changing exchange rates.

Budapest

I'd like a single room/double room.	Egyágyas/Kétágyas szobát/kérek.
with bath/with shower	fürdőszobával/ zuhanyozó val
What's the daily rate?	Mibe kerül naponta?

AIRPORT *(repülo"tér)*

International flights arrive and depart from modern **Budapest Ferihegy Airport 2**, 38 km (24 miles) east of the capital. Terminal A is used by Malév (the Hungarian national airline) and Terminal B by all other airlines. Both terminals have car rental agencies, money exchange desks, ATM machines and information offices.

It takes about 45 minutes to get from the airport to the center of Budapest. **Airport Taxi** (Tel. 341-0000) charges a fixed (but expensive) price to the city (4,800 Ft to Pest). The **Airport Minibus** (Tel. 296-8555) is a much better deal; it will deliver you to any address in Budapest (1,800 Ft one-way, 3,300 Ft roundtrip). Look for the prominent "Airport Minibus" sign at the information desk. For the minibus return journey to the airport, call 24 hours in advance to book and allow plenty of extra time — as much as an additional hour — in case of delays. The **LRI Airport Centrum** bus (Tel. 296-8555) travels from the airport to Erzébet tér (by the Kempinski hotel and metro station), departing every half hour from 5:30am to 10pm, for just 800 Ft each way (pay on board). Allow about 45 minutes travel time. There is also a **public airport bus** (BKV Plusz Reptér busz) — the cheapest but least convenient method of transport from the airport — that travels to the Kõbánya-Kispest metro station.

Airport Information: Tel. 296-9696.

B

BUDGETING FOR YOUR TRIP

Though prices have risen dramatically in the past five years, Budapest remains inexpensive for most visitors from Western

Europe and North America relative to other European capital cities. Still, visitors expecting the dirt-cheap Central Europe of the very recent past may be in for a bit of a surprise. Budapest's four- and five-star hotels are now nearly as costly as those in Western Europe. Many facets of daily life remain true bargains for visitors: the highly efficient public transport system; hearty food and drink served in a *borozó* (wine bar) or *sörözo* (beer hall); coffee and cakes in elegant Victorian coffee-houses; and museums and concert performances.

Transportation to Budapest. For most Europeans, Budapest is a short, fairly inexpensive flight or train ride away. North Americans (and of course Australians, New Zealanders and South Africans) can expect their flights to eat up considerably more of their budgets — anywhere from $500 to $1000 or more, though off-season roundtrip deals on Málev from New York and Canada can sometimes be had for as little as $300.

Accommodation. Budapest hotels at the top levels charge almost as much as you would expect to pay in other European capitals. For a double room in high season, in central Budapest (prices in euros): 5-star hotel over €200; 4-star hotel €140–200; 3-star hotel €90–140; 2-star hotel or panzió €50–90 or less.

Meals and drinks. Dining out in Budapest remains a bargain except at the most upscale and famous restaurants, where you may pay close to New York or London prices. A three-course meal for two, with wine and service, in a moderate restaurant should cost 3,000–7,500 Ft; at an expensive restaurant, allow 7,500-10,000 Ft or more.

Local transportation. Public transportation is very cheap. A single ride on bus, tram, metro, or HÉV suburban railway is just 100 Ft. Only taxis are relatively expensive. Opt for public transportation except in rare instances (after-hours), and always call for a taxi rather than hail one on the street.

Budapest

Incidentals. Museum admission: 100–500 Ft. Entertainment: theater, musicals, classical music concerts range from 700–4,000 Ft, though certain performances at the Hungarian Opera House can cost up to 8,000 Ft. Excursions and tours: walking and city tours range from 2,400 Ft to 7,500 Ft, and Danube or Balaton trips from 16,000 Ft to 20,000 Ft.

CAR RENTAL (See also DRIVING)

Arrangements and conditions for car rental are similar to those in other countries. The minimum age requirement is 21 and you must have been in possession of a valid license for at least one year.

Car rental is fairly expensive: Daily rates, including unlimited mileage, range from $25–$40 a day for an economy-size car, including CDW insurance. At press time, gasoline cost 225 Ft per liter. If you pay with a credit card, in theory you should not be assessed the hefty 25 percent AFA tax. Ask if CDW insurance is included in the price. Local agencies, such as **Budget Hungary** (Tel. 214-0420; discount with Budapest Card) are usually the cheapest, but the major international agencies, including **Avis** (Szervita tér 8; Tel. 318-4158), **Budget** (Krisztina körút utca 41–43; Tel. 214-0420), and **Hertz** (Hotel Marriott, Apáczai Csere János utca 4; Tel. 266-4361) have offices at the airport and in downtown Pest.

CLIMATE

Budapest is very cold in winter and swelters in sticky July and August. The best weather (and the best time to visit) is from May to early June and September to October. The chart below shows Budapest's average daytime temperature:

	J	F	M	A	M	J	J	A	S	O	N	D
°C	-2	0	6	12	16	20	22	21	17	11	6	1
°F	29	32	42	53	61	68	72	70	63	52	42	34

CLOTHING

Dress is not formal in Budapest, but Hungarians are increasingly style-conscious, and chic Western fashions are much in evidence. Evening gowns and jeans are both acceptable at the egalitarian Opera House. Casinos and top-echelon restaurants expect smart attire.

CRIME AND SAFETY (See also EMERGENCIES and POLICE)

As Western European capitals go, Budapest is a safe place. However, petty crime — almost unheard of in the Communist days — is on the rise. As far as visitors are concerned, the major crime is pickpocketing (usually on the Metro, trams and buses) or car theft. You should have nothing to fear if you take the usual precautions, especially on Váci utca and the Castle Hill district, both very much frequented by tourists.

Violence against tourists remains rare and most city streets are safe at all hours (though you should exercise caution at night in the areas immediately around the main railway stations). A few scams are commonly directed at unsuspecting tourists. One is propagated by prostitutes (usually prowling on Váci utca), who invite men to have a drink in a nearby bar. You can count on the bar tab to be preposterously inflated (or worse, led to the nearest ATM machine for a forced cash withdrawal). Another, rarer, scam involves people claiming to be police officers and demanding to inspect your currency — both Hungarian and foreign — to guard against fake bills. In such a case, do not produce your money to be inspected. Insist that you be taken either to the police station or your embassy. That is usually enough to ward off the imposter-thief.

Report any theft to the Tourist Police Office (Vigadó u. 6, 24 hours) and get a copy of your statement for your own insurance purposes. There is a crime hotline: Tel. 438-8080 (English and German spoken).

Avoid dealing with black-market money-changers, as this is a criminal offence (see MONEY).

CURRENCY RESTRICTIONS

Visitors may be required to report an equivalent of 50,000 Ft or more in cash if the amount is taken out on departure. As for Hungarian currency, foreign nationals may bring in 350,000 Ft.

I have nothing to declare.   **Nincs elvámolni valóm.**

CUSTOMS and ENTRY REQUIREMENTS (See also EMBASSIES AND CONSULATES)

All visitors require a valid passport to enter Hungary. The citizens of many countries, including most European nations, the US, Canada and South Africa, do not need a visa. However, citizens of Australia and New Zealand do. Visas, good for 90 days, can be obtained from any Hungarian diplomatic mission; this usually takes 24 hours.

DRIVING (See also CAR RENTAL)

To take your car into Hungary you need a valid driving license and automobile registration papers. Cars from most European countries (including the UK, Germany, and Austria) are presumed to be fully insured, so no extra documentation need be shown. To be safe, carry proof of insurance.

Road conditions. Hungary has one of the highest accident rates in Europe. Budapest drivers are notorious for their recklessness. Central Budapest boulevards are many lanes wide and you have to contend with trams and trolley buses as well as heavy traffic.

Hungary's expanding motorway system is well-maintained and toll-free. Yellow emergency telephones are spaced every 2 km (1½ miles) along the Budapest–Balaton–Vienna M7 highway. Avoid this road on Sunday nights in summer, when it is at its busiest.

Rules and regulations. Drive on the right and pass on the left, but be careful at all times. Cars must be fitted with a nationality plate or sticker. A set of spare bulbs, a first-aid kit, and a warning triangle are also obligatory. Seat belts are compulsory in front and back seats; children under 12 are prohibited from travelling in the front seat. Motorcycle riders and passengers must wear crash helmets. Using a cellular phone while driving is prohibited. There is no tolerance for drinking and driving; any amount of alcohol in the bloodstream is a punishable violation.

Speed limits are 120 km/h (75 mph) on highways, 100 km/h (62 mph) on major roads, 80 km/h (50 mph) on country roads, and 50 km/h (31 mph) in built-up areas, with on-the-spot fines for speeding.

Fuel (*benzin*). Filling stations are common along highways and main roads, but don't venture down minor roads without filling up. Stations are usually open 6am–10pm; there is 24-hour service in the populated areas. Unleaded fuel is widely available (about 225 Ft/liter). Credit cards normally accepted for petrol payment.

Parking. Parking is a major problem all over town, with drivers scrambling for meters and the totally inadequate number of parking spaces. If you are driving, check that your hotel has parking facilities. A car parked in a prohibited zone will be towed away.

If you need help. Remember to put out the red warning triangle 50 m (165 ft) behind your car. All accidents must be reported within 24 hours to the Hungária Insurance Company (Tel. 372--5377). If anyone is injured, the police must be notified. Cars with damaged bodywork are allowed out of the country only if they have an official certificate for the damage.

The **Hungarian Automobile Club** operates a 24-hour international breakdown service in Budapest (Tel. 345-1755).

Road signs. Standard international pictographs are in use all over Hungary. Motorways are indicated by green signs, all other main roads by dark blue.

Budapest

Fluid measures

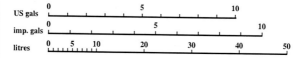

Distance

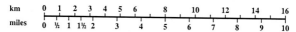

Full tank, please.	**Kérem, töltse tele a tankot.**
Check the oil/tyres/battery, please.	**Kérem, ellenorizze az olaljat/a gumikat/az akkumulátort.**
I've broken down.	**Meghibásodott a kocsim.**
There's been an accident.	**Baleset történt.**
Can I park here?	**Szabad itt parkolnom?**

ELECTRICITY

The current is 220-volts throughout Hungary. Plugs are the standard continental (2-pin) type, for which British and North American appliances need an adapter. Electrical equipment of 110V/60Hz requires an adapter or voltage converter.

EMBASSIES and CONSULATES (*nagykövetség; konzulátus*)

Australia: XII., Királyhágo tér 8-9; Tel. 457-9777.

Canada: XII., Budakeszi út 32; Tel. 392-3360.

Ireland: V., Szabadság tér 7; Tel. 302-9600.

New Zealand: VI., Térez körút 38, 4th floor; Tel. 331-4908.

UK: V., Harmincad utca 6; Tel. 266-2888

US: V., Szabadság tér 12; Tel. 475-4400.

EMERGENCIES (See also Embassies and Consulates, Health and Medical Care, Police, and Crime and Safety)

Emergency telephone numbers throughout Hungary:

General Emergency	**112**
Ambulance	**104**
Fire	**105**
Police	**107**

24-hour medical service (English-speaking): Tel. 200-0100

G

GAY and LESBIAN TRAVELERS

Budapest has one of the largest and most active gay communities in Central and Eastern Europe. There is a monthly gay listings magazine, *Mások* ("*Others*"), gay radio programs and a monthly gay erotic magazine. As *Mások* suggests, though, Budapest's gays and lesbians are not yet wholly accepted by the mainstream community. The age of consent for gay sex is 18 in Hungary; sexual contacts between heterosexuals are allowed from 14. A **gay hotline** (Tel. 0630/932-3334, English and German spoken) and Web site (<gayguide.net/Europe/ Hungary/ Budapest>) serve the gay community.

Gay hangouts include the Király and Rács thermal baths (especially Saturday afternoons) and the following nightspots (only a few of many): Mystery Bar-klub, V., Nagysándor József utca 3; Jácint Eszpresszó, V., Október 6 utca 5; Darling, V., Szép utca 1; Club 93, VIII., Vas utca 2; and Angyal Bár, VIII., Szövetség utca 33, *the* gay dance club in Budapest.

GETTING THERE

Air travel. Scheduled service operated by the Hungarian National Airline, Malév, departs daily from London to Budapest with two flights per day (the flying time is just over 2 hours). Scheduled flights are also available from British Airways. Malév flies direct to Budapest every day except Friday from New York (9–10 hours) and operates a partnership with Delta Airlines. Malév also flies nonstop from Toronto to Budapest every Tuesday (additional flights during summer months). Flights to the Hungarian capital originate in most major European cities. Occasionally it pays to fly to Vienna and then board a train to Budapest.

International airport. International flights arrive and depart from modern Budapest Ferihegy Airport 2, 38 km (24 miles) east of the capital.

Rail travel. Budapest can easily be reached from any major European city. From the UK, trains depart from London's Victoria station daily, arriving at Budapest some 28 hours later. The most direct route is via Dover to Ostend and Vienna. Prague and Vienna are the most common connecting points. The following international rail passes are valid in Hungary: InterRail, Euro Domino, EurailPass (and its variants), European East Pass, and Hungarian FlexiPass. In the US Tel. (800) 4 EURAIL.

Budapest has two international railway stations, **Keleti** and **Nyugati** (both have metro stations attached).

By car/coach. Budapest is connected by major highways to Berlin, Prague, and Vienna. The cheapest way to get from London to Budapest is by coach, which takes some 31 hours. If you plan to drive across the Continent, the most direct route is via Ostend, Brussels, Cologne, Frankfurt, Linz, and Vienna. Budapest is about 1,730 km (1,080 miles) from London. Buses from Western Europe arrive at the Erzsébet tér station (Tel. 485-2162); from Eastern Europe, the Népstadion station (Tel. 252-1896).

By hydrofoil. From April to the end of October, a hydrofoil service (Mahart) operates daily along the Danube from Vienna to Budapest (with a stop in Bratislava). The trip takes five hours one way and the price is quite reasonable. For information in Budapest, Tel. 484-4025; in Vienna, Tel. 431/729-2161.

GUIDES and TOURS

Three-hour city tours are offered by **Cityrama** (Tel. 302-4382); **IBUSZ** (Tel. 317-7767), and the curiously named **Queenybus** (Tel. 247-7159). Tickets range from 5,500 to 6,900 Ft. Danube Bend tours are on offer through IBUSZ and other travel agencies. The most popular are Szentedre/Visegrád/Esztergom; Szentendre alone; and Danube evening cruises. Excursions farther afield visit Lake Balaton and the Great Plain for riding and folklore shows.

Walking tours of special interest include **Absolute Walking Tours** (Tel. 30/211-8861; <www.budapestours.com>; and **Paul Street Tours** (Tel. 20/958-2545; <www.firsteuropeanshipping. com>). Tours of Jewish Budapest are conducted by **Chosen Tours** (Tel. 355-2202) and the Municipality of Budapest, which leads "**Jewish Heritage**" walking tours (Tel. 317-2754). Audio-tape guides are available for hire at the National Museum and the Open Air Village Museum near Szentendre.

H

HEALTH AND MEDICAL CARE (See also EMERGENCIES)

Hungarian doctors and other health officials are in general knowledgeable and skilled. Most speak English and German. Tap water is perfectly drinkable in Budapest.

If you have an accident or are suddenly ill, the Hungarian National Health Service (abbreviated Sz. T. K.) and the emergency squad (Mentok) are well-equipped to handle such problems. Emergency medical treatment on the scene is free for foreigners; all other treatment has to be paid for at the time you receive the service. Ask at your hotel desk or consulate for the name of a doctor who speaks your language.

The **American Clinic** is located in district I., Hattyú utca 14 (Tel. 224-9090). For 24-hour medical care, call **Falck SOS Hungary** (II., Kapy utca 49/B; Tel. 200-0100), which has an ambulance service.

Budapest

Pharmacies. Look for the sign gyógyszertár or patika. In Hungary these shops only sell pharmaceutical and related products. (For cosmetics and toiletries you'll need an illatszerbolt or drogéria; for photo supplies a fotószaküzlet.) The Budapest Sun and Tourinform carry lists of night pharmacies. Among them are **Teréz Patika** (Teréz krt. 41 (Tel. 311-4439) in district VI.; and the one at Frankel Leo utca 22 (tel. 212-4406) in Buda II.

Where's the nearest pharmacy?	**Hol a legközelebbi patika?**
I need a doctor/dentist.	**Orvosra/Fogorvosra van szük ségem.**
I have a pain here.	**Itt fáj.**
a fever	**láz**

HOLIDAYS (*hivatalos ünnep*)

1 January	*újév*	New Year's Day
15 March	*Nemzeti ünnep*	National Holiday (Anniversary of 1848 Revolution)
April (moveable)	*Húsvét hétfo*	Easter Monday
1 May	*A munka ünnepe*	Labor Day
June (moveable)	*Whitsun*	Pentecost
20 August	*Szt István ünnepe*	St. Stephen's Day
23 October	*Nemzeti ünnep*	Remembrance (Republic) Day
25 December	*Karácsony elso napja*	Christmas Day
26 December	*Karácsony második napja*	Boxing Day

INTERNET CAFÉS

Ami (V., Váci utca 40; Tel. 267-1644; daily, 9am–2am).

Cyber Café (Café Eckermann) (VI., Andrássy út 24; Tel. 374-4076; Monday–Friday 2–10pm, Saturday 10–10pm. (Metro: M1 Opera)

Easynet Internet Center (V., Váci utca 19-21; Tel. 485-0460; daily, 10am–11pm).

Vista Kávéház (Paulay Ede utca 7; Tel. 267-8603; Monday–Friday 10am–10pm, Saturday 10am–8pm, Sun 10am–6pm).

LANGUAGE

Hungarian, wholly unrelated to the languages of the surrounding countries (it is classified in the Finno-Ugric family of languages, along with Finnish and Estonian), is the mother tongue of 95 percent of the population. It continues to baffle linguists and those who wish to learn it. Hungarian is notoriously difficult.

Many Budapestis speak German, though English is quickly gaining ground and is more popular than German among the young.

One source of confusion (among many) is how to address a Hungarian. The surname always precedes the Christian name; Westerners would say or write Károly Jókai, whereas Hungarians say Jókai Károly. Second, there is no direct equivalent of Mr or Mrs; the nearest terms, which are very formal, are *Uram* for Mr and *Hölgyem* for Mrs. You can mix East and West by saying, for example, Mr Jókai.

Here are a few useful phrases and some signs you are likely to see:

Yes/no	**igen/nem**
please	**kérem**
Good morning	**Jó reggelt**
Good afternoon	**Jó napot**
Good night	**Jó éjszakát**
Goodbye	**Viszontlátásra**
Thank you	**Köszönöm**
Do you speak	**Beszél angolul/**
English/French/German?	**franciául/németül?**

Budapest

entrance/exit	**bejárat/kijárat**
pull/push	**húzni/tolni**
open/closed	**nyitva/zárva**
Good day (formal)	**Tó napot**
Hi (informal, singular/plural)	**Szia/Sziasztok**
How are you? (formal/informal)	**Hogy van/Hogy vagy?**
Very well thanks, and you?	**Köszönöm, nagyon jól, és ön?/**
(formal/informal)	**Köszönöm, nagyon jól, és te?**
shop	**bolt/üzlet**
department store	**áruház**
pharmacy	**gyógyszertár**
post office	**posta**
theater	**színház**
railway station	**pályaudvar**
open	**nyitva**
closed	**zárva**
entrance	**bejárat**
exit	**kijárat**
road	**út**
street	**utca**
square	**tér**
boulevard	**körút**
bridge	**híd**

MAPS

Both Tourinform and IBUSZ offices supply visitors with free maps of the city that are sufficient for most purposes. You should also pick up a Budapest Transportation Authority map (BKV térkép), available free at Metro stations. If you want a more comprehensive map, look for the *Cartographia Budapest City* or *Budapest Atlas* maps of Budapest, available in bookstores.

MEDIA

Newspapers and magazines. The two recommended English-language weekly papers are the *Budapest Sun*, which features an excellent "What's On" section and *Budapest Business Journal*. Western newspapers, including *The International Herald Tribune*, *The Financial Times* and *USA Today*, arrive the day of publication. Others may arrive a day later. *Where Budapest?* (in English) is the essential monthly magazine for finding out what's on. It is free and available through hotels and tourist information offices. *Pesti Est* has comprehensive listings of nightlife activities.

Radio and television. English news can be heard every full hour between 5am and 10pm at Radio Bridge (FM 102.1 MHz). There are many Hungarian TV channels. One of the oldest — MTV 1 — shows *BBC News* on Monday to Friday evenings (times vary — see the *Budapest Sun* for details). All hotels with four or more stars (and some three-star hotels) offer satellite television.

MONEY

Currency. The unit of currency is the forint (Ft). Coins in circulation are 1, 2, 5, 10, 20, 50, and 100 Ft. Banknotes come in denominations of 100, 200, 500, 1,000, 2,000, 5,000, 10,000 and 20,000 Ft.

Currency exchange. Foreign-exchange offices are found in most banks, hotels, larger campsites, travel agents and large shops. Banks and some travel agencies offer the best rates. Don't forget to take your passport when you want to change money. It's wise to keep all your exchange receipts until you leave the country.

Don't be tempted by the numerous offers you get on the street from black-market money-changers. It is illegal to deal with them and you may well be cheated.

Credit cards. Visa, Mastercard, and American Express are increasingly accepted in hotels, restaurants, and shops, but are not accepted everywhere. In some establishments, only one type of credit card is accepted. Supermarkets, museums, and train stations expect payment in cash.

ATMs. Cash machines (PLUS and Cirrus networks) are widespread in Budapest, especially in the Inner City (downtown Pest). They dispense cash in Hungarian forint.

Traveller's checks. These may be cashed at all of the above outlets and may sometimes be used as cash, though you will almost certainly get a poorer rate of exchange than if you convert them to cash. Commission is generally 1 to 2 percent.

OPEN HOURS (See also HOLIDAYS)
Most businesses in Budapest are open Monday–Friday, 8am–5pm. **Shopping centers** are open Monday–Saturday, 10am–9pm, Sunday, 10am–6pm. Smaller **shops** are open Monday to Friday, 9 or 10am to 6 or 7pm and Saturday 9 or 10am to 1 or 2pm. Some close all day Saturday. For 24-hour shopping look for the sign "Non-Stop." **Banks** are open 8am–3pm, Monday–Friday (some close at 1pm on Friday). **Museums** are closed on Monday and open 10am–6pm Tuesday–Sunday. **Post offices** are open Monday–Friday, 8am–6pm, Saturday, 8am–1pm. There are two 24-hour offices (see POST OFFICES).

POLICE (*rendőrség*) (See also CRIME AND SAFETY)
Police wear blue-and-gray uniforms. Traffic police also wear white caps and white leather to make them more visible. During July and August, tourist police also patrol the streets with translators.

Police:	Tel. 107
Budapest Police Headquarters:	Tel. 343 0034
Where is the nearest police station?	**Hol a legközelebbi redőrség?**

POST OFFICES (*postahivatal*).

Post offices (Magyar Posta) handle mail, telephone, telegraph, telex, and (at the larger offices) fax. Stamps (*bélyeg*) are best bought at tobacconists or where postcards are sold. Most hotels will stamp and post your mail for you. Postboxes are painted red.

Local post offices and the main post office at Petőfi Sandor utca 13-15 (metro: Deák tér) are open from 8am to 5 or 6pm Monday to Friday and from noon to 2pm on Saturday. Other branches include: Nyugati Train station (Teréz körút 51-53; open 7am–9pm, Sunday 8am–8pm); Keleti Train station (Baross tér; open 7am–9pm, closed Sun); and Castle Hill Post Office (Dísz tér 15; open 8am–4pm Mon–Fri).

International postcards cost 107 Ft to Europe and 117 Ft to the US. Letters (20g) cost 157 Ft to Europe and 167 Ft to the US.

DHL, Federal Express and UPS have offices in Budapest.

express (special delivery)	**expressz küldemény**
airmail	**légiposta**
I'd like a stamp for this letter/postcard please.	**Kérek egy bélyeget erre a levélre/a képeslapra.**
I'd like to send a telegram.	**Táviratot szeretnék feladni.**

PUBLIC TRANSPORTATION

The Budapest Transport Authority (BKV) operates an extensive, cheap, clean, and reliable system. Throughout central Budapest, you're never more than a few minutes' walk of a bus, tram, or metro line, and waiting time is rarely more than a few minutes. Maps of the whole network are available from major metro and railway stations.

You can buy a single ticket (*jegy*), in a strip of 10, or save yourself the bother of having to validate them on each trip by buying a 1, 3, 7, or 14-day pass (you'll need a passport-sized photo for the latter two). A ticket is valid for a single unbroken ride of any distance on any service. You must buy a ticket before boarding. They are sold at all stations, travel bureaus, and tobacconists.

Budapest

Most public transport runs between 4:30am and 11:30pm. There are a limited number of night buses and night trams (look for the suffix é on their number). Don't forget to validate your ticket by punching it in the red machine (passes don't need validating). These are located on board buses and trams, and for trains on line 1 of the metro. On metro lines 2 and 3 you have to use the orange machines just inside the station entrance. BKV ticket inspectors, wearing red armbands, patrol public transportation and are very vigilant. Foreigners tend to be targeted along with youths. Fare dodgers have to pay an on-the-spot fine (1,500 Ft).

Current fares and additional information are available at <www.BKV.hu>.

City transport

Buses (*busz*). A bus stop is marked by a blue-bordered rectangular sign with the letter M and a list of stops on the route. Signal that you want to get off by pressing the bell.

Mini-buses. A convenient mini *várbusz* service runs an almost constant shuttle between Moszkva tér and Dísz tér (next to the funicular railway) on Castle Hill, stopping every 200 meters.

Trams (*villamos*). Yellow trams, or streetcars, usually in trains of three to four carriages, cover a 190-km (120-mile) network; some run throughout the night. Trams 4 and 6 are especially effective for following the Outer Ring (or Nagykörút) and trams 47 and 49 follow the Inner Ring.

Taxis (*taxi*). Budapest's taxi-drivers are notorious for overcharging foreigners, and unless you're laden with luggage or have some other reason for not traveling on public transport, they should be avoided.

If you do want a taxi, call one of the following firms: Fõ taxi (Tel. 222-2222), Radio Taxi (Tel. 377-7777), or Volántaxi (Tel. 266-6666).

Taxis can be hailed in the street when the "taxi" roof sign is lit, but hailing a cab is not recommended. If you do, make sure the meter is working (and set at zero before you set off), or agree on the fare in advance.

Subway or underground (*metró*). The metro operates three lines. The M1 line (yellow) opened in 1896 and is a museum piece, though still effective. The only point where the original line converges with the two newer lines (M2, red, and M3, blue) is at Deák tér station. Remember you have to use a new ticket each time you change lines (a problem solved by buying a pass; see above). A single ticket costs 100 Ft.

Transport outside the city

Coaches. Coaches to the airport, other parts of Hungary, and European destinations run from the Erzsébet tér station. Buses to the Danube Bend leave from Árpád station. Information on coach services: Tel. 485-2100.

Trains. There are three HÉV suburban commuter lines of which only the Batthyány tér to Szentendre (via Aquincum) service is likely to be of interest to tourists.

Inter-city trains operate from three Budapest stations: **Keleti** (Baross tér; Tel. 333-6342; most international trains), **Nyugati**

(Nyugati tér; Tel. 349-8503; mostly destinations east), and **Déli** (Alkotás u; Tel. 355-8657; domestic).

The main **MÁV ticket office** for national and international trains is located at Andrássy út 35 (Tel. 461-5400 or 461-5500).

A special treat for train enthusiasts are the **nostalgia trains**, vintage and steam locomotives run by MÁV Nosztalgia (Tel. 428-0180 or 302-3580; <www.miwo.hu/old_trains>) that go to the Gödöllö Palace, the Hungarian Plain, Danube Bend, and Eger. The "Royal Hungarian Express" visits the cities of the Austro-Hungarian Monarchy (Budapest, Prague, and Vienna).

River transport. Pleasure boats run to and from the Danube Bend in the summer season, departing from Vigadó tér piers 6/7. Hydrofoils also run to Esztergom and Vienna (Tel. 317-2203).

R

RELIGION

The majority of Hungarians are Roman Catholic. Mass is usually said in Hungarian, but in some churches it is said in Latin, English, or German. Other faiths, notably Protestant, Eastern Orthodox, and Jewish, are also represented.

Where Budapest and *The Budapest Sun* publish details of services in the city held in English and other languages.

T

TELEPHONE (*telefon*)

Public phones accept 10, 20, and 50 Ft coins or phone cards. Most public phones now are phone-card only. Phone cards (800 or 1800 Ft) may be purchased at newsstands, tobacconists, post offices and some hotels. Long distance and international calls can also be made through the Belvárosi Telephone Center (V., Petõfi Sándor utca 17; open 8am–8pm Monday to Friday, 9am–3pm Saturday and Sunday).

Making a local call from your hotel may not be as costly as in other countries, as local phone charges are quite cheap.

To make an international call from a public phone, dial the international access code (00), followed by the country code and telephone number, including the area code. There are no off-peak rates. For national calls beyond Budapest, dial the national access code (06), followed by the area code and number. A local call within Budapest has 7 digits; it is not necessary to dial the area code. Mobile telephone numbers have 11 digits.

For international directory assistance Tel. 199.

TIME ZONES

Hungary follows Central European Time (Greenwich Mean Time + 1 hour, or US Eastern Standard Time + 6 hours). In summer the clock is put one hour ahead (GMT + 2).

Summer time:

New York	London	**Budapest**	Jo'burg	Sydney	Auckland
6am	11am	**noon**	noon	8pm	10pm

TIPPING

Tipping is the norm in Hungary. It is customary to leave 10 to 15 percent at restaurants and round up the bill at bars. Some restaurants may add on a 10 percent tip; look carefully at the bill and ask if this appears to be the case to avoid tipping twice. Porters, maids, toilet attendants, Gypsy violinists playing at your table, masseurs at thermal baths, and tourist guides also expect tips.

TOILETS

In Budapest all public toilets are pay toilets. Some cafés may even charge patrons for use of their facilities.

Férfiak	men's room
Nők	women's restroom
WC (*"vay-tsay"*)	toilet

Budapest

TOURIST INFORMATION (*turista információs iroda*)

Tourist information is dispersed among several entities. **Tourinform**'s main offices are V., Vigadó utca 6 and Sütō utca 2, near Deák tér metro station (Tel. 317-9800; <www.hungary-tourism.hu>). The Vigadó office is open 24 hours; Sütō, daily 8am-8pm. It also has an office in the Nyugati Railway Station (Tel. 302-8580) and Tárnok utca 9–11 on Castle Hill (Tel. 488-0453). The main **Tourism Office of Budapest** is located at VI., Liszt Ferenc tér 11 (Tel. 322-4098; <www.budapestinfo.hu>).

A 24-hour **tourist information hotline** is maintained (Tel. 438-8080).

The main **IBUSZ office** is at Sütō utca 2, 50 m (165 ft) from the Déak tér metro station. Another office is Ferenciek tere 10 (Tel. 485-2700). IBUSZ is also a major tour operator, providing a booking service and selling excursions. Hours are 8am to 5:30pm Monday–Friday. There is a 24-hour IBUSZ branch at Petofi tér 3 (Tel. 318-5707).

Before you leave home, you can write to the **Hungarian National Tourist Board** for general information:

UK: Hungarian National Tourist Office, 46 Eaton Place, London SW1 X8AL. Information: Tel. (020) 7823-1055 fax (020) 7823-1459.

US: Hungarian National Tourist Office, 150 East 58th Street, New York, NY 10155; Tel. (212) 355-0240, fax (212) 207-4103; <www.gotohungary.com>.

WEB SITES

<www.traveltohungary.com>
<www.gotohungary.com>
<www.budapestinfo.hu>
<www.budapest.com>

<www.hungarianhotels.com>
<www.hotels.hu>
<www.budapesthotels.hu>

WEIGHTS and MEASURES

Length

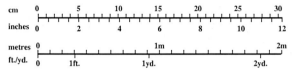

Weight

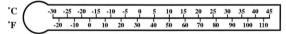

Temperature

Y

YOUTH HOSTELS (*Ifjúsági szállás*)

There are about a dozen youth hostels in Budapest. You can pick up a list of addresses at Tourinform or visit the Travelers' Youth Hostels information center (Tel. 343-0748; open daily 7am–11pm) at the Keleti train station. Recommended hostels include **Back Pack Guesthouse** (XI., Takács Menyhért utca 33; Tel. 209-8406; <www.backpackbudapest.hu>) on the way toward Buda; the spectacularly situated **Citadella** (XI., Citadella sétany; Tel. 466-5794; <www.besthostel.hu>); and **Diáksport** (XII., Dózsa György út 152; Tel. 340-8585), a Mellow Mood hostel.

Recommended Hotels

Hotels in Hungary are graded from one star to five stars. Budapest's stock of quality visitor accommodation has improved but choices are limited, especially at the lower end of the range. It is always wise to book ahead, particularly for September, New Year, Easter, and the first or second weekend in August, when the Hungarian Grand Prix is staged. High season on Lake Balaton is from Easter to September and during peak times demand is such that some establishments offer only a half-board arrangement.

The following guide denotes the rack rate price of a double room with bath/shower in high season (May through October, as well as Christmas) including breakfast and VAT. Hotel room rates, especially at the upper end, are usually quoted in euros (€), though some do so in US dollars. All accept major credit cards, except where noted.

For assistance finding a room upon arrival, contact **Tribus** (V., Apáczai Csere János u. 1; Tel. 318-3925), a 24-hour location service. They have lists of private accommodations, as does **IBUSZ** (V., Ferenciek tere 10; Tel. 485-2767).

$	less than €50	US$56
$$	€50–90	US$56–80
$$$	€90–140	US$80–158
$$$$	€140–200	US$158–225
$$$$$	more than €200	US$225

BUDA — CASTLE HILL & VIZIVÁROS

Budapest art'otel. $$$ *Bem rakpart 16-19; Tel. 487-9487, fax 487-9488; <www.parkplazaww.com>.* The newest addition to the scene (July 2000) is the city's most chic hotel, designed in high modernist style by Donald Sultan, the American contemporary artist. Half the hotel fronts the river, with spectacular views of the Danube and Parliament; the remainder occupy huge rooms created from former fishermen's houses. Rooms are contemporary, with original artwork and funky, colorful touches. Good value given its style and service; perfect for hipsters and the visually oriented. Cool restaurant (Chelsea). Wheelchair access. 27 rooms.

Hilton $$$$+ *Hess András tér 1-3; Tel. 488-6600, fax 488-6925; <hiltonhu@hungary.net>*. One of the most luxurious hotels in town, with arguably the best location — atop Castle Hill, with views over the Danube (rooms facing the river are more expensive). You'll either love or hate the hotel's modern incorporation of a 13th-century Dominican church. Business center, *söröző* (beer hall), casino. Wheelchair access. 322 rooms.

Kulturinnov $$ *I., Szentháromság tér 6; Tel. 355-0122, fax 375-1886; <mka3@mail.matav.hu>*. Tucked inside a handsome Renaissance building just steps from the Matthias Church, this small hotel's location is unbeatable. Rooms are basic and small, unlike the grand central staircase and arches of the entrance, but a very good deal for the center of Castle Hill. 18 rooms.

Carlton Hotel $$$ *I., Apor Péter utca 3; Tel. 224-0999, fax 224-0990; <www.hotels.hu/carlton>*. A ten-year-old hotel, newly renovated and renamed under Austrian ownership (it used to be the Alba). It sits at the foot of Fisherman's Bastion and close to Clark tér on the river side, but set back from busy Fö utca on a quiet alleyway. Comfortable and well-appointed, with 4-star aspirations. No restaurant. 95 rooms.

Hotel Victoria $$$ *Bem rakpart 11; Tel. 457-8080, fax 457-8088; <www.victoria.hu>*. A small but modern hotel facing the river along the Buda side. Rooms are large, if in need of a style makeover, but service is friendly and the price excellent for this location and these views. Restaurant. 27 rooms.

THE REST OF BUDA

Gellért **$$$$** *XI, Gellért tér 1; Tel. 385-2200, fax 366-6631; <www.danubiusgroup.com/gellert>.* You can't get any more famous than the legendary Gellért, at the foot of the hill of the same name, opposite the Liberty Bridge in Buda. Its magnificent thermal baths get most of the attention, but the art nouveau hotel has tons of character. Traditional rooms are furnished with antiques and are very comfortable. Most rooms have balconies overlooking the river and excellent views of all Budapest. Guests get free access to baths and pools. Helpful staff, excellent restaurant and coffee shop. Business center, baths and pools, *sörözo* (beer hall), nightclub. 234 rooms.

Citadella **$** *XI., Citadella sétány; Tel. 466-5794, fax 386-0505.* Spartan but clean budget accommodation within the old castle on Gellért Hill. Some rooms have magnificent views. Coach invasions by day, tranquility by night (unless student groups are resident). Restaurant and *borozó* (wine bar). 12 rooms.

ÓBUDA

Corinthia Aquincum **$$$$** *III., Árpád Fejedlem útja 94; Tel. 436-4100, fax 436-4156; <wwwcorinthia.com>.* A modern addition to the spa-hotel scene, this thermal bath hotel (built 1991) is located by Margaret Bridge. The décor is modern, though with a Roman theme. Full spa and balneotherapy facilities, including a swimming pool, sauna and fitness room. Good connections for public transport. Nightclub, business center and typically Hungarian *sörözo* (beer hall). Wheelchair access. 312 rooms.

BUDA HILLS

Panoráma Hotel and Bungalows **$$** *XII., Rege ut 21; Tel. 395-6121, fax 395-6245.* A 19th-century Alpine-style chalet in the Buda Hills (access via cog-railway or bus 21), but only 7 km (4 miles) from Castle Hill. Country-style bungalows are also available within the hotel's 3-hectare (1.2-acre) grounds, ringing the pool. Swimming pool, sauna, solarium, *sörözo* (beer hall). 35 rooms.

Molnár Panzió $$ *XII., Fodor utca 143; Tel. 395-1873, fax 395-1872; <www.hotel-molnar-hu>.* This pair of modern chalet-style houses enjoys a picturesque setting on the hillside known as Széchenyi mountain, 15 minutes from the city center and within easy reach of the M7 motorway. Bedrooms are unusual and individually styled and impeccably clean; one has a large tub, another a nice terrace. Restaurant, bar, and pleasant outdoor terrace. 23 rooms.

Petneházy Country Club $$$ *II., Adyliget Feketefej utca 2-4; Tel. 376-5992, fax 376-5738.* Perfect for sporting types, located 10 km (6 miles) from the center of town at the foot of the Buda Hills. "Rooms" are actually individual wooden cabins, each with a sauna, kitchen and porch. Club facilities include swimming pool, solarium, tennis courts, and riding club. Wheelchair access. 45 rooms.

MARGARET ISLAND

Grand Hotel Margitsziget $$$$ *XIII., Margitsziget; Tel. 452-6200, fax 452-6262; <www.danubiusgroup.com>.* The fin-de-siècle "Grand Old Lady" of the island was built in 1893 and renovated in 1987 (the interior is modern). Ensconced in trees, many rooms have terraces with views of the park. Business center, swimming pool, full balneotherapy facilities, fitness room, *sörözo* (beer hall). No air-conditioning. Wheelchair access. 152 rooms.

PEST EMBANKMENT

Hyatt Regency Budapest $$$$$ *V., Roosevelt tér 2; Tel. 266-1234, fax 266-9101; <www.budapest.hyatt.com>.* The spectacular 10-story glass atrium not only has a wall of plants, but also a hanging prop plane. The rooms are furnished in a contemporary but comfortable style with stupendous views across the river; the night views of the illuminated Chain Bridge and Castle Hill nearly justify the prices. Business center, nightclub, casino, *sörözo* (beer hall), indoor pool, sauna, solarium, fitness room. Wheelchair access. 351 rooms.

InterContinental $$$$$ *V., Apáczai Csere János utca 12-14; Tel. 327-6333, fax 317-9808.* This former "AmEx Hotel of the Year" receives particularly high praise for the quality of its staff and its superb restaurant. Rooms have excellent work desks and can be outfitted with computer and printer. Riverfront rooms cost 10 percent more. Business center, fitness center, indoor swimming pool, sauna, solarium. Wheelchair access. 398 rooms.

Marriott Budapest $$$$ *V., Apáczai Csere János utca 4; Tel. 266-7000, fax 266-4343; <www.marriott.com>.* This huge concrete building, built in the 1960s, looks much better from the inside. Every luxuriously appointed room enjoys splendid views to Castle Hill, and many have small balconies. Excellent restaurant, business center, fitness center, indoor swimming pool, sauna, solarium, sun-terrace, squash court. Good selection of restaurants and a winning buffet dinner. Wheelchair access. 362 rooms.

INNER CITY PEST

Astoria $$$ *V., Kossuth Lajos utca 19; Tel. 484-3200, fax 318-6798; <www.danubiusgroup.com/astoria>.* An elegant turn-of-the-century atmosphere still pervades at Budapest's oldest hotel. Though it could use another updating, it has the Old World charm — period furnishings and Persian rugs — that many will find perfectly in synch with their expectations of Old Europe. The Astoria is situated on a major traffic junction; guests are advised to request a room at the back. Rooms are spacious and comfortable. Restaurant. 130 rooms.

Kempinski Hotel Corvinus $$$$$ *V., Erzsébet tér 7-8; Tel. 429-3777, fax 429-4777; <www.kempinski-budapest.com>.* In terms of architecture, this is the most striking — and most costly — of the city's modern 5-star hotels. It has extremely elegant guest rooms and public areas. The large rooms are amenity-laden with phones in bathrooms, heated floors and towel racks. The business traveler's top choice is undergoing a room renovation to keep up with new competitors like the Meridien next door. Popular *sörözo* (beer hall), business center, indoor swimming pool, sauna, solarium, boutiques, fitness center. Wheelchair access. 369 rooms.

Le Meridien Budapest $$$$$ *V., Erzsébet tér 9-10; Tel. 429-5500, fax 429-5555; <www.lemeridien.com>.* Budapest's newest ultra-luxe hotel is stunning and stately, occupying a pre-war building, for half a century the old police headquarters. Rooms are large and handsomely and soothingly furnished. Public rooms glitter with chandeliers. As if an outright challenge to the city's previously most luxurious hotel, Le Meridien moved in right next door to the Kempinski (for the moment, the newer hotel is a better deal). Fine restaurant, business center, swimming pool, sauna, solarium, boutiques, fitness center. Wheelchair access. 218 rooms.

Starlight Suiten $$$ *V., Merlég u 6; Tel. 484-3700, fax 484-3711; <www.starlighthotels.com>.* This stylish mid-size modern hotel is a German initiative, located very near Roosevelt tér and the Chain Bridge, the location is excellent. Rooms are colorful and sunny, and all are suites. Good value. Tennis court, business center. 54 rooms.

Taverna $$$$ *V., Budapest, Váci utca 20; Tel. 485-3100, fax 485-3111; <www.hoteltaverna.hu>.* This tall, 12-story hotel is wedged into a narrow space on Budapest's famous shopping street, and its location is its central appeal. Standard but well-equipped rooms, friendly service. Popular with European groups. Fitness center, sauna, solarium, excellent formal restaurant (Gambrinus), *sörözo* (beer hall). 226 rooms.

OUTER PEST

Radisson Béke SAS $$$$ *VI., Teréz körút 43; Tel. 301-1600, fax 301-1615;<www.radisson.com/budapesthu>*. This long-established hotel is located within a grand old building, which was renovated to form a luxury hotel in 1985. Handy location near the Nyugati Train Station. Superb coffee shop. Business center, casino, café, indoor swimming pool, solarium, sauna, fitness room. Wheelchair access. 247 rooms.

Liget $$–$$$ *VI., Dózsa György út 106; Tel. 269-5300, fax 269-5329; <hotel@liget.hu>*. The Liget is a modern-style hotel located on a busy boulevard on the edge of the City Park, very near to Heroes' Square, several good restaurants, the zoo and the Szechenyi baths. Friendly staff, pleasant bedrooms. Only the wing facing the main street has air-conditioning. Sauna, solarium. 139 rooms.

Mercure Hotel Budapest Nemzeti $$$ *VIII., József körút 4; Tel. 477-2000, fax 477-2001; <www.hungary.com/pannoinia/ nemzeti>*. The sky-blue façade of the once-famous National, built in the 19th century, looks out cheerily onto busy Blaha Lujza square. It was renovated in 1987 but has retained its art nouveau styling. Bedrooms are spacious and functional. Request one facing the inner courtyard to save yourself from sleepless nights. *Sörözo* (beer hall), chic restaurant. 76 rooms.

LAKE BALATON

Auróra $ *Bajcsy-Zsilinszky utca 14, Balatonalmádi; Tel. (88) 338-810, fax (88) 338-410*. This 14-story hotel enjoys a quiet location in a park on top of a small hill with excellent views in all directions. The lake is just a few minutes' walk away, and the hotel has its own private beach. Facilities include an indoor swimming pool, sauna, solarium, ten-pin bowling alley, tennis courts (nearby), nightclub. 240 rooms.

Recommended Restaurants

The Budapest dining scene has improved dramatically in recent years, and diners now have a wider choice of cuisines and types of restaurants to eat in than ever before, including Korean, Greek, vegetarian, Mexican, Middle Eastern, Russian, Japanese, Indian and, of course, Hungarian.

Book ahead wherever possible, especially at top-tier restaurants. Many restaurants stay open throughout the afternoon. The only time when restaurants are likely to be closed is Sunday night.

All the restaurants below accept major credit cards *except where noted*. In Hungary, menu prices generally do not include service. However, check your bill, as some restaurants automatically add a 10 percent gratuity. The following guidelines denote the average cost of a three-course meal for two, excluding wine and service:

$	less than 3,000 Ft
$$	3,000-6,000 Ft
$$$	6,000-9,000 Ft
$$$$	over 9,000 Ft

BUDA — CASTLE HILL & VIZIVÁROS

Alabárdos $$$$–$$$$$ *Országház utca 2; Tel. 356-0851. Open Mon–Sat for lunch and dinner.* A grand 15th-century mansion with elegant furnishings and fittings. The updated Hungarian menu is long and the well-prepared dishes are served on beautiful Zsolnay porcelain. Reservations and formal attire required.

Aranyhordó $$ *Tárnok utca 16; Tel. 356-1367. Open Mon–Sat for lunch and dinner.* This famous old eating house is actually a small dining complex that includes a *sörözo* (beer hall), a café, and a stylish restaurant, all set in an attractive 14th-century building. The specialties include *fogas* (pike-perch from Lake Balaton). Guests are serenaded with Gypsy music.

Arany Kaviár $$$ *Ostrom utca 19; Tel. 201-6737. Open daily for dinner only.* Down the hill towards Moszkva tér, this small, cozy Russian restaurant is a good place to sample generous portions of caviar with blinis at reasonable prices. The rest of the menu, specializing in fish, features Russian items and more typical Hungarian fare.

Belgian Brasserie $$ *I., Bem rakpart 12; Tel. 201-5082. Open daily 12pm–12am.* This good-natured restaurant facing the riverbank on the Buda side is notable primarily for its outstanding selection of Belgian beers. It is also a good place to eat mussels and Belgian frites, as well as other well-prepared, simple and affordable dishes.

Fekete Holló $$$–$$$$ *Országház utca 10; Tel. 356-2367. Open daily 11am–12am.* Set on a relatively quiet part of this popular street, the "Black Raven" has a small, cheerful outdoor terrace and an attractive 18th-century dining room. If you want a truly exotic meal, try the pancakes with caviar followed by roast wild boar.

Tabáni Kakas $$$ *Attila út 27; Tel. 375-7165. Open daily for lunch and dinner.* Fowl is the specialty at Tabáni Kakas, an old neighborhood favorite situated behind Castle Hill. Dishes include steak tartare and crispy fried goose leg with red cabbage and mashed potatoes. Peaceful atmosphere with piano music.

ÓBUDA

Kehli $$$$ *Mókus utca 22; Tel. 250-4241. Open Mon–Fri for dinner, Sat–Sun 12pm–12am.* Kehli is a small, wood-paneled local tavern with a long-standing gourmet tradition. For a truly different and delicious meal, start with bone-marrow, then try one of the house pork specials, and finish with a Transylvanian Golden Galushka pastry. Lovely summer courtyard. Accordion music. Closed Sunday.

Kisbuda Gyonge $$$ *Kenyeres utca 34; Tel. 368-6402; Open Mon–Sat for lunch and dinner.* A charming restaurant that oozes fin-de-siècle ambience with period furnishings and old photographs. If you haven't tried goose yet, this is the place to try the impressive and challengeing "Hungarian goose feast".

PEST — INNER CITY

Apostolok $$ *Kigyó utca 4–6; Tel. 318-3559. Open daily 12pm–12am.* The Apostolok, housed in a converted 19th-century church, is one of the most atmospheric eateries in the city. It serves typical Hungarian cuisine — try the mutton stew soup, pork cutlets ragout, or suckling pig with cabbage.

Articsóka $$–$$$ *VI., Zichy J. utca 17. Tel. 302-7757. Open daily 12pm–12am.* A few blocks from the Opera House, this large, airy and cheerful Mediterranean restaurant serves simple Greek, Spanish and Italian fare, with occasional Hungarian dishes mixed in. There's a nice terrace and lively crowd, many of whom spill into the restaurant from the performance space at the back.

Baraka $$ *V., Magyar utca 12–14. Tel. 483-1355. Open Mon–Sat 10am–12am. No credit cards.* This new initiative, around the corner from the historic Astoria hotel, is among the most delightful new restaurants to hit Budapest. The project of an expat American and his Israeli wife, Baraka is chic but understated: It has deep red walls, candlelight and a two-level central space dominated by large paper hanging lamps. Good wines by the glass. Creative international menu, dishes very nicely prepared and presented. Recommended are the chopped Arabic salad and veal medallions with asparagus in cherry shallot sauce. Homemade desserts are outstanding.

Centrál Kávéház $–$$ *Károlyi Mihály utca 9. Tel. 266-2110. Open daily 8am–12am; Fri & Sat until 1am.* This legendary café, opened in 1887 and finally reopened after nearly a half century's dormancy, is a great place for a good, affordable meal any time of the day. Serves soups, salads, sandwiches and more elaborate meals, and a great selection of cakes and pies for dessert.

Café Kör $$ *Sas utca 17. Tel. 311-0053. Open Mon–Sat, 10am–11pm. No credit cards.* An informal and fashionably low-key little restaurant near Deák tér, Café Kör is one of those places you find yourself returning to again and again. It has warm Roman orange walls, light hardwood floors and vaulted ceilings, and the staff speaks excellent English. A long list of daily specials is hand-written on butcher paper (many items get crossed off by night's end). If it makes an appearance, you might try roasted goose liver with apples, cranberry and parsley potatoes. Nice list of wines by the glass. Open for breakfast.

Gerbeaud $$$ *Vörösmarty tér 7. Tel. 429-9000. Lions Fountain open Mon-Sat lunch and dinner, Sun lunch only; Pub, open daily 11am–12am, Fri–Sat 11am–2am.* The café is legendary, but Gerbeaud is much more than just cakes and cappuccino. For a full sit-down meal, choose between the elegant, atrium-like **Lions Fountain Restaurant** (entrance on Harmincad utca), a lovely fine-dining experience, especially when candlelit at night, or head to the bustling basement for the charming **Sörház** (Gerbeaud Pub), an old-fashioned beer cellar that brews its own beer.

Kárpátia $$ *Ferenciek tere 7–8; Tel. 317-3596. Open daily 12pm–11pm.* A "must-see" tourist brasserie and restaurant with spectacularly ornate turn-of-the-century décor. Very reasonably priced traditional Hungarian and Transylvanian menu including some set-price meals. The summer courtyard is in the courtyard of a former monastery. Live Gypsy music.

Légrádi & Társa $$$–$$$$ *Magyar utca 23; Tel. 318-6804. Open Mon–Sat for dinner.* This tiny, elegant restaurant — sumptuously decorated with oil paintings and antique furniture — is one of the city's most fashionable eating places, offering an international/ Hungarian menu for well-to-do romantics at dinner. Food is served by tail-coated waiters on Herend china with silver cutlery. The formal atmosphere is quiet, with guitar music.

Lou Lou $$$ *Vigyázó F. utca 4. Tel. 312-4505. Open Mon–Fri for lunch and dinner; Sat dinner only.* A chic and intimate French bistro in the financial district of Pest. Dishes such as rack of lamb with haricot vert or grilled monkfish are prepared with care, and the presentation is superb. Nice wine list, including wines by the glass.

Mátyás Pince $$$ *Március tér 7; Tel. 318-1693. Open daily for breakfast and 11am–1am.* One of Pest's most popular tourist spots serves good traditional (but imaginative) Hungarian dishes in an atmospheric turn-of-the-century cellar setting. Those with a healthy appetite should try the King Matthias Platter. Gypsy music.

Merleg $ *Merleg utca 6. Tel. 317-6911. Open Mon–Sat, 8am–11pm.* A decidely untouristy take on authentic, home-style Hungarian cooking. It's the kind of place where you'll probably share a table and may have to point to one of the specials that are handwritten on a chalkboard. Not far from the Chain Bridge, on a quiet Pest side street.

Százéves Étterem $$$$ *Pesti Barnabás utca 2; Tel. 266-5240. Open daily 11am–12am.* This elegant Baroque-style establishment, Budapest's oldest restaurant is still going strong after a century of business. Renowned for its game (try venison with cranberry sauce) and dishes like tenderloin in Bull's Blood (the wine, that is). Excellent wine cellar. Summer terrace, Gypsy music.

Vegetárium $ *Cukor utca 3; Tel. 484-0848. Open Mon–Sat 11:30am–11:30pm.* The city's first and best vegetarian restaurant — recently reopened — offers a multi-ethnic, macrobiotic experience to please even the strictest vegans. Pleasant and relaxed New Age ambience with good service.

Budapest

Vörös és Fehér $$$ *VI., Andrássy út 41. Tel. 413-1545. Open daily 11am–12am.* Occupying prime real estate in Andrássy út, this fashionable, split-level bistro wouldn't be out of place in New York City. Run by the Budapest Wine Society, it has a massive wine list, including a dozen or more by the glass that change weekly. Choose from a daily list of international and Hungarian specials and a nice selection of tapas and soups.

CITY PARK

Bagolyvár $$ *XIV., Allatkerti út 2; Tel. 351-6395. Open daily 12pm–11pm.* The "owl's castle" is the little sister of famous Gundel, which is just around the corner. The difference is that Bagolyvár is much less formal and expensive, and it's staffed entirely by young women. It serves a limited but superbly cooked range of Hungarian family-style dishes, such as grilled meats and mititei (small sausages with baked green pepper) from a daily changing menu.

Gundel $$$$ *Allatkerti út 2; Tel. 321-3550. Open daily for lunch and dinner (and Sunday brunch).* Hungary's most famous and beautiful restaurant, founded in 1894, Gundel is a byword for Hungarian haute cuisine and the haunt of royalty and elites. Palatial and bathed in oil paintings, it features international as well as Hungarian gourmet delights, such as *fogas* (pike perch). Be sure to save room for the famous *palacsinta* (dessert pancakes). Reservations and jackets required.

Muzeum $$$ *12 Muzeum korut; Tel. 267-0375. Open Mon–Sat for lunch and dinner (and Sunday brunch).* An excellent place for a meal before or after visiting the huge and tiring National Museum next door, this longtime classic continues to present formidable, if not flashy, renditions of Hungarian traditional favorites. Such dishes as veal paprikas, pike perch and smoked trout are perfectly suited to the handsome Old World dining room.

Robinson $$$ *Városliget (City Park lake); Tel. 343-3776. Open daily for lunch and dinner.* The city's most idyllic and sylvan restaurant sits on its own island in the lake overlooking City Park and is perfect for outdoor dining. Excellent Hungarian and international cuisine in the restaurant, lighter meals served in the café and grill (open April to September). Guitar music.

OUTER PEST

Carmel Prince $$ *Kazinczy utca 31; Tel. 342-4585. Open daily 12pm–11pm.* This spacious Jewish cellar restaurant, decorated with photographs of Israel, is located in the heart of the Jewish Quarter, and has a long and interesting menu (though this is not kosher.). Goose is the house specialty.

Fészek Klub $ *Kertész utca 36; Tel. 322-6043. Open daily 12pm–1am.* Serving an encyclopedic menu of genuine Hungarian home-cooking in a pretty, charmingly dilapidated garden courtyard and frequented by a hip crowd. Try the "Reform" *bárány* (roast lamb), wild game and freshwater fish dishes.

Fausto's $$$ *Donhány utca 5; Tel. 296-6806. Open Mon–Sat for lunch and dinner.* Everyone's favorite Italian restaurant is this nicely decorated and low-key place right across the street from the Great Synagogue. It isn't cheap, but it can be counted on for excellent Italian standards and a nice wine list.

DANUBE BEND

Aranysárkány $$ *Vendéglo2 Szentendre, Alkotmány utca 1/a. Tel. 26/301-479. Open daily 12am–10pm.* A little place upstairs, easily overlooked on one of Szentendre's quaint streets, the "Golden Dragon" is a great place to take a breather from shopping and visiting artists' studios. Try the *szoljanka* soup, with cabbage and smoked meat, and the paprika peppers stuffed with pork and rice.

INDEX